Nicole

The true story of a
Great White Shark's
journey into history

RICHARD PEIRCE

DEDICATION

This book is dedicated to Nicole and to all the world's
Great White Sharks, and is written in the hope that
conservation efforts achieve a secure future for these
amazing and wonderful yet endangered animals.

Published by Struik Nature
(an imprint of Penguin Random House
South Africa (Pty) Ltd)
Reg. No. 1953/000441/07
The Estuaries No. 4, Oxbow Crescent,
Century Avenue, Century City, 7441
South Africa
PO Box 1144, Cape Town, 8000
South Africa

First published in 2017 by Struik Nature

10 9 8 7 6 5 4 3 2

Publisher: Pippa Parker
Editor: Helen de Villiers
Designer: Janice Evans
Cartographer: Liezel Bohdanowicz
Proofreader: Thea Grobbelaar

Reproduction by Hirt & Carter Cape (Pty) Ltd
Printed and bound by Times Offset (M) Sdn Bhd, Malaysia

Visit www.penguinrandomhouse.co.za and join
the Struik Nature Club for updates, news, events and
special offers.

● The images of sharks and fins in this book
are mainly for illustrative purposes and do not
necessarily portray Nicole; when they do, the
image is labelled accordingly.

● Every effort has been made to trace and
credit the owners of images used in this book
– we apologise if any have slipped in that are
unattributed or wrongly so.

Front cover image: Michael Scholl

Contents

Forewords

IN 1997 I LEFT MY FAMILY AND COUNTRY and moved to South Africa just three years after Nelson Mandela had swept to electoral victory as the head of the newly named 'Rainbow Nation'. At the time shark enthusiasts the world over had become acquainted with the names Dyer Island and Shark Alley thanks to a BBC Wildlife documentary, and the little town of Gansbaai on South Africa's southwestern coast was just beginning its journey to fame.

After I arrived in South Africa, there followed 10 blissful years of living and breathing (and sweating and laughing) *Carcharodon carcharias*, the Great White Shark. My move was timely because until then almost no research had been done on the species, which had recently been granted protection in South African waters. From my lounge window I could watch whales while drinking my coffee, and a half-hour boat ride took me to the waters around Dyer Island, and the largest population of Great White Sharks in the world.

I felt lucky and privileged, almost like an explorer from a bygone age, as I settled in and initiated a population study of these elusive and misunderstood animals. The internet had been born only a few years earlier, GoPros didn't exist even in the wildest geek dreams, and neither *National Geographic* nor *Discovery Channel* had started their shark broadcasting blitz.

It quickly became clear that identification tagging Great White Sharks had its limits, but as an avid photographer I soon realised that there was another way to identify individual sharks. Side-on shots of dorsal fins provided reliable fingerprint-style identification, and I continued this work for several years, refining it all the time.

Day after day I photographed and observed these 'hollow-eyed, man-eating, prehistoric monsters', and day after day their behaviour astonished me and dispelled the popular myths. They demonstrated individual behavioural traits showing different personalities and often exhibiting great curiosity. I observed social interaction, and the individual sharks were often very relaxed and seemed as interested in observing us as we were in watching them. It might sound far-fetched, but on many occasions when they spy-hopped and looked at us, I couldn't help thinking that if they had cameras, *they* would have been photographing us!

Those close to me are aware of my obsession with Nicole and many would use the word 'love' to describe the way I talk about her. For five years she was almost like a shark 'wife', as every year she came back to Dyer Island for a few months and presented her distinctive fin, swam curiously around my boat, and looked at me with her beautiful dark blue eyes. Little did I know when I first saw her in 1999 that she would become the most famous shark in the world and would help protect her species.

Shark Alley flows between Dyer Island and Geyser Rock.

Nicole's incredible story is one of survival and inspiration, but it is also the story of the humans who studied and came to know her and, as a result, now understand her species better. I have been friends with Dr Ramon Bonfil for many years, and each time we meet, Nicole is always part of the conversation. I will always be very thankful to him for having enabled our team of South Africa-based scientists to have access to satellite-tagging technology in those early days. Nearly two decades after I last saw Nicole, I have moved away from research and into conservation, and I still feel privileged to be living my dream by working at the Save Our Seas Foundation. The Foundation came into being shortly before Nicole was tagged, and in a way we continue to follow the example of her story by helping to fund research that leads to effective conservation.

Despite the innumerable documentaries that give the impression that we know everything there is to know about sharks, many of the 1,200 shark and ray species remain a complete mystery to us today. The Foundation supports education, research and conservation projects worldwide to help better understand these creatures that are so important for maintaining the delicate balance of our oceans.

Nicole is an extraordinary book. At one level it tells the simple tale of a fish that swam 22,000 kilometres – and yet it is also far more than that. Richard Peirce narrates Nicole's story in an interesting and compelling way, personifying her and leaving readers in little doubt that in some ways he considers her superior to humans.

For the rest of my life I will feel proud and privileged that I knew Nicole and played a part in telling her story to the world. My most precious dream is that she continues to roam our oceans and has not become a victim of man's destructive influence on our seas. I still fervently hope that someone, somewhere has taken, or will take, a photograph of her distinctive dorsal fin and will share it with me.

Michael Scholl
Chief Executive
Save Our Seas Foundation

The waters around Dyer Island are home to the world's
largest population of Great White Sharks.

If people find the image of a fin slicing through the water frightening, how much more ghoulish is the image of a fin being hacked off to put into a bowl of soup?

NICOLE IS THE AWESOME TRUE STORY of an amazing Great White Shark. In fact, awesome and amazing are hardly big enough words to describe her story. I have been fascinated by sharks since I was a little girl and *Nicole* ticked all my boxes; I couldn't put it down. Adventure, excitement, suspense, conservation and science are all part of this story.

Great White Sharks are an extraordinary species – they have been proved to be intelligent and are beautiful and powerful. When I was younger, 'shark' meant frightening images of fins gliding through the water. I guess fear is excitement so I became curious and started to learn all I could about these fish. When I discovered that sharks should be much more afraid of us than we of them because of the huge numbers being killed for their fins, I became hostile. My hostility was towards the fishermen and poachers who catch and kill these animals. My original frightening image of fins slicing through the water was replaced by the nightmare of fins being hacked off to put into bowls of tasteless soup.

My continuing research showed that no-one actually knows how many Great Whites are left in the world. What we do seem sure of is that they are endangered and so need our help and protection in all the oceans where they occur.

I have been very fortunate to have dived with Great White Sharks, and it saddens me to think that if I have children they might not be able to do the same.

Reading this story has made me realise how independent and self-sufficient these amazing creatures are, and what extraordinary inbuilt capabilities they have, whereas we have to rely on computers and electronics. I can't say more; it will spoil the story.

Charlotte Peirce-Gregory
(Age 14)

Acknowledgements

The Nicole story has long fascinated me; the dilemma was how to turn the 22,000-km journey of one fish into an interesting tale. Finally, here's the result – but without the help of the following it could not have been done: Fiona Ayerst; Dr Ramon Bonfil; Neil Britton; Andy B. Casagrande; Wilfred Chivell; Brenda du Toit; D. Ebert, S. Fowler & L. Compagno – authors of *Sharks of the World* (Wild Nature Press, 2013); Chris Fallows; Heather Fener; Sarah Fowler; Denise Headon; Ali Hood; Dr Ryan Johnson; Yvonne Kamp; Alison Kock; Deon Kotze; Ruby-Gay Martin; Sharon Martin; Johanri Meyer; Mike Meyer; Dr Les Noble; Jacqueline Peirce; Charlotte Peirce-Gregory; Thomas Peschak & Michael Scholl – authors of

A shark spotter's
view of a Great
White Shark

South Africa's Great White Shark (Struik Publishers, 2006); Lalo Saidy; Dirk Schmidt – author of *White Sharks*; Michael Scholl; Harry Stone; Stephan Swanson; Alison Towner; Henriet van Rhyn and Birgitta Weaving.

Special thanks must go to Michael Scholl and Ramon Bonfil who gave generously of their time, enabling me to put the story together; to Harry Stone who, although not involved in the story, provided many of the photographs free of charge; to Heather Fener for many of the expedition photos; and to anyone who may have slipped through the net – my apologies and thanks.

Thanks are also due to The Shark Trust in the UK, and The Book Cottage and The Windsor Hotel, both in Hermanus, South Africa.

And finally, thanks to all at Struik Nature who once again dealt with a difficult author with patience, and did a brilliant job putting this book together – Pippa Parker, Helen de Villiers, Janice Evans and Belinda van der Merwe.

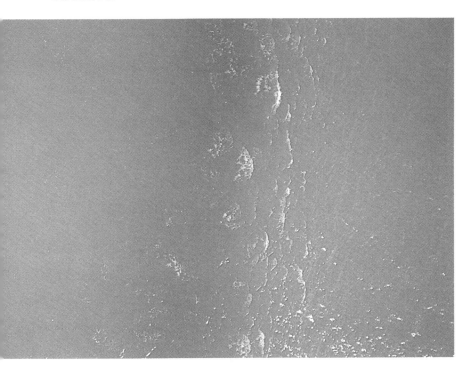

GREAT WHITE SHARK FACTS

- The Great White Shark's scientific name is *Carcharodon carcharias*
- Female Great White Sharks are larger than males and can reach 6 metres in length
- Great Whites can swim at speeds of up to 40 kilometres per hour
- Great Whites' conservation status is Vulnerable
- South Africa is one of the world's Great White hot spots
- Great Whites have sharp, triangular, serrated teeth
- Great White Sharks are found throughout the world's oceans, mostly in cool waters close to the coast
- Great Whites have a grey/brown top side and a pure white belly, which gives them their name
- A Great White has over 300 teeth in its mouth
- Great Whites generally feed on seals, sea lions, cetaceans (small whales, dolphins, etc.) but NOT humans
- Great Whites are both ambush predators and search patrollers
- Great White Sharks produce between two and 13 pups per litter
- Great Whites are at the top of the ocean food chain, but are endangered as a result of overfishing by humans
- Research now indicates that Great Whites may live for up to 70 years

- Great Whites are cartilaginous, i.e. they do not have a bony skeleton
- Great White Sharks, Makos, Threshers and Porbeagles are all warm-blooded
- Great Whites do not survive in captivity
- Great Whites are known to stick their heads out of the water, which is called spyhopping
- Great Whites will produce and lose over 30,000 teeth in their lifetime
- The number of Great White Sharks is unknown but it might be as low as 3,000
- Great Whites are protected by the Convention on International Trade in Endangered Species and by many countries, including South Africa, the United States and Australia
- Great Whites are the most feared sharks, but Tiger and Bull sharks probably attack more people
- Great White Sharks are also called White Pointers, White Sharks, and White Death
- The pressure of a Great White Shark's bite is one of the most powerful in the animal kingdom
- At the time of writing (2016) no-one had seen a Great White mate or give birth

Introduction

After breakfasting she moved slowly along the beach, her every movement a symphony of beauty, grace, economy and power: a queen in command of all she surveyed. She exuded the confidence, indeed almost the arrogance, possessed naturally by those who know they are the coolest thing around.

here the sandbank met the shore she veered left towards a huddled, early morning group of potential admirers. When you know you will turn heads you don't have to hurry, and her slow progress merely underlined her confidence. Lithe, supple and poised, she drew admiring glances as she approached – intakes of breath and wows as cameras started to click. A slight change of course brought her right alongside the group, and as she slid smoothly past them, a backward glance would have reassured her that her audience was still watching.

She turned and passed a second time before sauntering off as if she had done her bit for the world for today. Actually, she had noticed another group of potential admirers about 200 metres away, which had just arrived and, like a queen on a walkabout among her subjects, the Great White Shark swam alongside the new arrivals.

The researcher was late waking up. He cursed this lapse until he remembered that the weather forecast had been bad, and so he had decided on a lie-in. For him a lie-in didn't mean a late, lazy start, it meant getting up at 06h30 instead of 05h30.

As he stumbled around, going through his start-of-the-day rituals – shaving, dressing, coffee making – he wondered when he would see the shark again. Lying in bed last night, he realised he had become obsessed; sharks were all beautiful, but she was special, and without making a sound she sometimes seemed to talk to him.

The thought of perhaps seeing her again lifted the gloom of the grey, windy day. Being captivated by a beautiful creature means highs and lows: a hollow, empty feeling of disappointment on days when you don't see her, and elation when you do – when she passes so close by, she thrills you to the core. He was hurrying now as he tidied up the kitchen and left the house.

If you are a scientist, your life, work and actions are supposed to be governed by logic and fact. To most people, having an obsession with potentially dangerous apex predators, and wanting to get as close as possible to them, would be considered illogical and incomprehensible. The scientist was unconcerned with what people thought; he had devoted his life to pushing the boundaries of knowledge about the creatures that had fascinated him since he was a child. As the years went by and his research deepened, and the list of his published scientific papers grew, he found answers to many questions; but the irony was that finding answers often just led to more questions. And it was this revolving process that drove him on his continuous voyage of discovery.

A trio of two humans and one shark were on a collision course. And when they met, their story would captivate the world, change scientific thinking and help protect a species from being driven to extinction.

CHAPTER ONE

The Great White Shark

Humans have feared and demonised sharks since earliest times. The very mention of the word 'shark' arouses fear and loathing out of all proportion to the impact these magnificent fish have on our lives. And until recently, there has been little understanding of the devastating impact we have on theirs.

'Shark' has long been a word that sends shivers down the human spine.

harks often feature prominently in the art and mythology of cultures that have strong ties to the sea. In the Cook and Solomon islands sharks are worshipped; they appear in Australian aboriginal mythology, play a central role in many Polynesian legends, and Hawaiians and Tahitians believe dead relatives can return in the form of sharks. In the Mediterranean, sharks also feature in the ancient literature of both Rome and Greece. In the 5th century BC, Herodotus related how shipwrecked Persian sailors were eaten by sharks; and around 330 BC, Aristotle wrote in detail about sharks in his *Historia Animalium*, accurately describing the differences between them and bony fish.

By the start of the 20th century sharks were firmly established as fearsome and loathsome predators. Shipwreck incidents in both world wars confirmed this view. When the USS *Indianapolis* was sunk in the Far East at the end of World War II, 900 men went into the water, but only 317 survived the sharks and the elements. Thereafter, the shark's pre-eminence as a figure of loathing equalled that of any monster before or since.

'Shark' has long been a word that sends shivers down human spines, and of all sharks, the Great White is the most feared. In recent years shark advocates, conservationists and scientists have made strenuous efforts to persuade the world's public that their fear of sharks is largely irrational. These efforts have mostly been in vain: despite the facts, despite logic and statistics, the luridly sensational *Jaws*-type headlines persist, and the stereotypical image remains intact.

Why is it proving so difficult to change the way sharks are perceived? The thought of a shark attack hits three basic human terror buttons, and appeals to our most deep-seated fears: of being out of our habitual element, of a hidden monster lurking somewhere out there, and of being eaten alive. *Jaws* is often fingered as a major culprit in giving sharks their killer image; it certainly hits all three buttons, leaving audiences stunned but riveted – although it's clear that sharks were portrayed as monster killers long before Benchley wrote his book, or Spielberg made the film.

To the three fear buttons we have to add the place of the shark in history, and the fact that we nurture a perverse yen for monsters and for horror. A visit to any fairground reveals such 'attractions' as *House of Horrors*, *Wall of Death*, *Spooky Monsters,* etc. Completely absent is any sign of *The House of Love*, *The Happy Room* or *Beautiful Creatures*! History, our basic fears, and our predilection for monsters will probably forever unfairly condemn sharks to being regarded as mindless killers.

Reaching lengths of over 6 metres, and with large, slash-like gills, Great White Sharks are among the planet's most awe-inspiring creatures. There are records of very large Great Whites in the Mediterranean, and one theory is that the biblical tale of Jonah and the whale should perhaps more correctly be titled *Jonah and the Great White Shark*.

Perhaps the world's best-known Great White Shark viewing area is around South Africa's Dyer Island.

Shark enthusiasts from all over the world flock to the Dyer Island area.

Great Whites are mainly distributed throughout the world's temperate seas. However, being semi-warm-blooded, they can to some extent regulate their body temperature, which increases their range into subtropical and cold oceans. Great Whites are now Red Listed by the International Union for the Conservation of Nature (IUCN) as 'Vulnerable'. Although Great White populations are seriously depleted due to overfishing, they still exist in various hot spots, among which are off the coasts of South Australia, California and South Africa. Perhaps the world's best-known Great White viewing area is around South Africa's Dyer Island, 8 kilometres offshore of the small town of Gansbaai, which styles itself 'The Great White Shark Capital of the World'.

Dyer Island is now firmly established on the South African tourist map. Every year shark enthusiasts, thrill seekers and tourists flock to the

Most people leave Gansbaai having become committed shark fans.

area to see one of the most iconic creatures on the planet. Eight operators work out of the little harbour of Kleinbaai (next to Gansbaai), and offer up to three trips a day taking people out to see the sharks. Many people are initially nervous of getting into the cages that allow safe viewing of sharks. Whatever their initial attitude, be they terrified, excited, bored or ambivalent, most people leave having become committed shark fans. They have met the rock stars of the ocean, and are rarely disappointed. Furthermore, no cage divers leave Gansbaai without having been made aware of the plight of sharks in general, and of Great Whites in particular.

In the mid-1980s marine scientists started to realise that many shark populations were under threat. As the new millennium dawned these concerns were becoming more widely accepted as fact, and were shared across the marine world, and well publicised in the media too. In 1991 the work of international expert Dr Leonard Campagno and others led to the Great White Shark being listed as protected by the

South African government. This was a precautionary measure and it was the first time a shark had been given protection based on the precautionary principle.

The main threat to sharks was their overfishing to meet the ever-increasing demand for shark-fin soup. The Chinese economy was booming and the rapidly expanding, newly affluent middle class had an appetite for the traditional luxuries previously denied them. Sharks were the losers: once a by-catch of other fisheries, they were now being targeted in their own right as tens of millions were harvested each year, primarily for their fins.

Each headline seemed to be trying to outdo the previous one: 30 million sharks killed each year; 70 million and even 100 million. Without solid baseline data, the extent of their overfishing was not known, nor how fast they were possibly being pushed to extinction in some areas.

We now know that the Great White Shark is particularly vulnerable to overfishing due to its late sexual maturity and its low reproduction rate. However, compared to many other marine species, sharks were, until recently, poorly researched; and at the time this story starts, Great White Shark research was in its infancy.

Paul Suter

The main threat to sharks is their overfishing in order to meet the demand for fins for shark-fin soup.

Image sourced through White Shark
Ventures, photographer unknown

Many people are
initially nervous
of getting into the
cages that enable safe
viewing of sharks.

CHAPTER TWO

Gansbaai – Walker Bay

Just as dawn was breaking over a silver sea, the female Great White Shark was patrolling the channel between Dyer Island and Geyser Rock. She was an impressive creature. She had a gunmetal grey topside, a brilliant white belly, she measured over 3 metres, and her large triangular dorsal fin sliced through the water as she made her lazy way along the beach.

t was an opportunistic run that she didn't really expect would yield breakfast, but as she was leaving the channel she picked up a scent trail and followed it. It was a young seal that had earlier been bitten by a large adult male and was now bleeding, dazed and disorientated. It thought it was heading back to the colony on Geyser Rock but actually was moving the opposite way, towards the beach.

The engine that is her tail propelled the shark faster and faster through the water, her eyes appeared to roll back in her head, her jaws opened and, for the little seal, it was all over. Great White Sharks are efficient feeders, and efficient users and converters of energy. The shark hadn't expected this surprise breakfast, and now she wouldn't need to eat for several days. She swam on from where she had eaten the seal, in the direction of the beach.

For the last four years she had followed an annual travel pattern that brought her to the Dyer Island area every year in early July, which is winter in southern Africa. Initially, the area had confused her as there were often lots of scent trails that led not to meals, but to bulky, noisy objects on the surface. She regularly followed the chum slicks to the cage-diving boats, and occasionally was fast enough to beat the person on the bait line and secure a small meal. At this time of the year she worked quite a large local area from Cape Agulhas to Walker Bay, and was a regular visitor to the Gansbaai cage-diving boats.

Two weeks ago she and over 20 other Great Whites had feasted on the carcass of a dead Southern Right Whale 18 kilometres south of Danger Point in Walker Bay. She had gorged herself and her full belly made her look pregnant.

Feasting on the whale may have saved her life. Several hours later, after leaving the carcass, she had picked up lots of interesting messages. The steady throb of an engine, blood and oily scents, and the signals of struggling fish. Curiosity, rather than a desire to feed, compelled her to investigate. The fishing vessel had deployed 10 kilometres of longline, and there was a wide variety of marine life either struggling on hooks, or already dead. Seabirds, dolphins, lots of Blue Sharks, Albacore, Tuna, Mako

Feasting on the
whale may have saved
the shark's life.

A dead whale – part of the bounty of the ocean, where nothing is
left to waste but rather fuels the rhythms of life-and-death.

Sharks, small Great Whites and others waited to be hauled in. She swam
past a large pregnant Blue Shark slowly moving in the final throes of its
death dance as it lost its battle with the hook and its life ebbed away.

She had encountered longlines before, but luckily something had
always put her off going for a bait. On this occasion the dead whale
had filled her to bursting point and she was not in feeding mode. She
swam up the line and approached the boat; then the steady throb of the
motors and a patch of engine oil annoyed her, and made her leave the
sad scene of death and devastation. Revulsion, fear, survival instinct or
something made her dive quickly to over 50 metres, and she continued
on her southwesterly course, heading back to the Dyer Island area.

Her mother had been a very large shark measuring well over 5 metres in length, and 1½ metres deep from top to bottom at her midpoint. She was a truly magnificent specimen, and was of a size now only rarely seen as a result of overfishing by trophy and commercial hunters. She had died 3 kilometres off Pringle Bay after an epic two-hour struggle with a sports angler. The angler towed his catch back to shore so that he could be photographed as the mighty victor! The oceans had lost a breeding-age predator from a species soon to be declared 'vulnerable', and the angler had gained a photograph and a good story. Somehow, the equation didn't really balance. Before becoming 1,050 kilograms of dead meat, this shark had been an ocean voyager. She regularly followed a migration route up the coast of South Africa to the Mozambique Channel, and had also made much longer ocean journeys. Her inbuilt navigation systems enabled her to move about in the ocean's vastness with an accuracy that allowed her to arrive at precise destinations at times of her choosing. She had produced four pups the year before she was killed, and three had survived. Each pup measured 1½ metres, and the two females and single male had gone their separate ways at birth.

It was now some years later, and one of the females – now approaching maturity and with a belly full of Southern Right Whale – remembered nothing of her mother, brother and sister. But her experiences with longline fishing boats, fuel oil smells, loud mechanical noises and bright artificial lights were adding up to form a negative impression in her mind; her instinct now was to be extremely wary. Luckily, she had always encountered the longlines at or near fishing vessels, and experienced the negatives from a safe distance; several kilometres behind the vessel there were only hooks, often holding a meal, and clean ocean, and had she approached from this end before learning caution she could have become a victim. As an apex predator, she faced few natural threats in the ocean, but she was learning fast about the 'unnatural' threats posed by humans.

The abalone poachers made little noise as they unloaded their vehicles and placed their equipment on board their boat in preparation for a night's work.

They were on scuba, which gave them at least an hour to work underwater. They would use dive torches to augment the baleful silver of the full moon, which is often known as a 'poacher's moon'. Once they had reached the area where they had decided to work, they got into their kit and slipped over the side into the cold water. They descended to about 4 metres, then regrouped before kicking for the bottom, 6 metres below. Each man carried a dive knife with which he would shuck the abalone (remove their shell) underwater. The mesh bags in which they collected the abalone would, when full, weigh 80 kilograms and contain about 300 shelled animals. Yellow torch beams danced on the sea bed as they began to collect and shuck the prized sea creatures.

The Great White picked up the disturbance in the water and the faint lights in the distance and went to investigate. The poachers were intent on their task and too busy collecting abalone to realise they were being stalked by the ocean's most feared predator.

The full moon cast its light down through the water column and only slightly illuminated the humans working on the sea bed. The sea was calm and the water unusually clear, and above the poachers the surface danced as the moonlight created a shimmering mirror.

Instinct or sixth sense made the man at the rear of the group glance behind him. They had been underwater for an hour, and he was starting to get cold, but now the blood in his veins turned to ice. Three metres behind him, and less than 2 metres above, was a shark, seemingly on top of him. He didn't try to warn his friends, didn't take evasive action, and he almost forgot to breathe. His mind and body froze as the Great White swam over him and towards his friends. They, meanwhile, were so intent

The full moon cast its light down through the water column.

on what they were doing they didn't notice the predator until after she had passed them. Then, aghast as they realised what had just passed them, they watched her disappear into the dark water. Columns of bubbles seemed to tow the divers to the surface; in their haste, they had forgotten that they had been under for an hour and should have surfaced more slowly to decompress. Heads broke the flat silver surface together, and for seconds there was no sound except for laboured breathing.

Not one of them had the presence of mind to put his face back in the water to check that the shark had actually gone. She hadn't, and now made another pass 5 metres below them, as she checked out these strange creatures for a second time. Her stomach was still full and so she was not hunting; she had merely investigated the bubbles and the commotion, and then decided against further investigation.

The divers didn't know it, but the dead whale had quite possibly saved at least one of them from serious injury or even death.

The Great White Shark had been back in the Gansbaai area for a week before finding the stricken seal pup, and would now stay in Walker Bay for several weeks more. It is easy to see why this area is, arguably, the world's leading Great White hot spot. Dyer Island is separated from Geyser Rock by a shallow channel known as Shark Alley. The island was originally called *Ilha da Fera* (Island of wild creatures) by 15th-century Portuguese seafarers; its name was later changed to Dyer Island after an American immigrant called Samson Dyer lived on it, collecting guano which he sold to farmers as fertiliser. On the other side of Shark Alley, Geyser Rock is home to a colony of around 60,000 Cape Fur Seals. Every year the colony produces 10,000–12,000 pups, of which most drown and only a small percentage survive to adulthood. Cape Fur Seals are the main prey species of the Great White Shark and are present around the island all year, but occur there in their largest numbers between May and September.

On this day in September 1999, as the Great White followed a chum slick towards the cage-diving boats, she knew nothing about what

would happen to her. Later, her life would change, and she would be on her way to becoming a global megastar – she would eventually be named Nicole, after a well-known Hollywood actress. She would come to represent a milestone in shark scientific research, and contribute to saving her species. Now, she swam at a leisurely 4 kilometres per hour towards her place in history.

Many tourists come to South Africa specifically to see Great White Sharks.

Dyer Island is separated from Geyser Rock by a shallow channel known as Shark Alley.

CHAPTER THREE

The researchers

When the two-year-old Mexican boy saw the sea
for the first time he said to his mother, 'Too much water,
Mom, too much water'. This event was hardly an
indicator as to how Ramon Bonfil would spend his life.
Six years later, Ramon's family moved to live by the
sea, and the young boy fell in love with the ocean
and the creatures that live in it.

Dr Ramon Bonfil

he deadly and the dangerous fascinate many a young boy, and Ramon was no exception; and of all the sea animals he got to know about, sharks captivated him the most. When he was 11, his aunt took him to San Diego Zoo, and when he saw his first real shark he was 'hooked' for life.

Studying marine biology was an obvious choice for Ramon at university, and he attended the Faculty of Marine Sciences of the Autonomous University of Baja California in Ensenada, Mexico. After graduating, his dream of a career studying sharks started to come true. His first job involved generating the basic information necessary for sustainable management of the Yucatan shark fishery. For the next five years, while working at the fishery, Ramon taught himself all he could about sharks. He then moved to the UK to do a marine biology Masters degree at Bangor University in Wales.

Several research projects and a PhD followed, and confirmed him as one of the leading shark experts in the world. In September 2001 Ramon went to work with the New York-based Wildlife Conservation Society (WCS), where his expertise in fisheries came into play, with a particular focus on sharks, tuna and billfish. His efforts were directed at conservation in the major fisheries management bodies in the USA and internationally. He travelled the world to meetings of the International Commission for the Conservation of Atlantic Tunas (ICCAT), the International Council for the Exploration of the Seas (ICES) and many other such bodies, promoting good science and science-based conservation.

Before joining WCS he had travelled to South Africa to attend the Indo-Pacific Fish Conference in Durban. Here, he met scientists who would later share with him in one of the most spectacular shark discoveries yet recorded.

Tiny landlocked Switzerland would not be an obvious place for one of the world's leading shark scientists and advocates to be born. While for many, Australia, South Africa and California conjure up images of the sea and sharks, Switzerland is usually associated with snow, chocolates

Ramon Bonfil   Michael Scholl   Ryan Johnson   Stephan Swanson

Olivier Born

Michael played a major role in restoring this exhibit in Lausanne Museum.

and banking. Michael Scholl was born in Zürich; he likes chocolate but not snow, and has little to do with bankers. He is, however, a committed shark enthusiast – and has been since he was 10 years old, when his parents gave him a book about sharks, and he visited a museum in Lausanne and gazed at the largest preserved Great White Shark in the world. This 5.9-metre giant was caught off the south of France and inspired a young boy's dreams, influencing his studies and ambitions. Later on, in a professional capacity, Michael Scholl would play a major role in restoring this magnificent exhibit.

In 1995 an advertisement at the University of Lausanne advertised a shark course for students at Bimini in the Bahamas. The course was

Michael Scholl in his element

to be run by the well-known and highly respected shark biologist, 'Doc Gruber'. Michael applied, was successful, and ended up making several visits to this, one of the world's most highly regarded 'shark schools'.

A marine biology degree at Aberdeen University followed, but the image of a Great White Shark that featured in the Lausanne museum kept reappearing in his mind. In 1997, a visit to South Africa was to prove instrumental in deciding Michael's future for the next few years. Apart from studies conducted at the Natal Sharks Board, very little research was being done on Great Whites at that time, and Michael saw both a need and an opportunity. When an invitation came to join Great White Shark authority, Craig Ferreira, as a researcher in Gansbaai, Michael jumped at it.

In 1998 New Zealander Ryan Johnson arrived in South Africa to continue his studies as a biologist. With its huge variety of both land and marine wildlife, Ryan found the lure of Africa irresistible and he enrolled at Pretoria University to do an Honours degree. Later, when he was trying to decide on a Masters degree, he came across an advertisement for a scientist to study the impact of cage diving, to assess how it affected Great Whites and whether it was causing conditioned behaviour and making them more dangerous to humans.

Ryan had lived by the sea all his life and during the year in Pretoria he realised how much he missed not being near the ocean. The job would require him to live on Dyer Island, surrounded by Great White Sharks. For some, this might sound lonely and daunting, but for Ryan, it was an invitation to paradise. He accepted the position, and it was the start of his career with Great Whites.

Ryan Johnson early in his research career

South African Stephan Swanson looks like an escapee from the Springboks rugby team. At 1.97 metres tall (6 foot, 4 inches), and with a build to match, he doesn't present an image to be argued with – even if you are a Great White Shark. He was born in Cape Town in 1966, and after finishing his studies, went to work for the Department of the Environment and Agriculture, in the marine section, which was then called Marine & Coastal Management (MCM). MCM were key players in all local marine research programmes.

The lives of Ramon, Michael, Ryan and Stephan, together with those of MCM's senior control technician Michael Meyer, research assistant Dean Kotze and chief technical engineer Michael Patterson, were all heading for a meeting with a very special Great White Shark and, together, they would make history, and as a result of their findings would help advance the protection of the species

The author (right) interviewing Stephan Swanson

43

South Africa's coasts have world-class beaches, and its waters are home to an enormously rich diversity of marine wildlife.

CHAPTER FOUR

A close encounter

The pilot had just told his passengers that they were on their final approach to Cape Town airport, and Table Mountain could be seen by those on the right-hand side of the plane. It was September 1997 and 25-year-old Michael Scholl looked out of the window and watched the ground and his new life rush up at him.

© Robin Sandry / Alamy / AfriPics

Table Mountain could be seen by those on the right-hand side of the plane.

n the terminal, waiting for his luggage, he looked around and wondered why everyone looked so glum. In contrast, Michael had a grin from ear to ear. He had accepted a position with the White Shark Research Institute, where he would spend the next few months researching and studying Great White Sharks, and he could think of nothing he would rather do, and nowhere he would rather be.

During his time with the Institute, Michael combined his interest in photography with his curiosity about sharks, and started taking side-on photographs of their dorsal fins. Every Great White's dorsal fin shape and markings are unique, so that a clear 90-degree, side-on photograph is therefore an accurate identification tool. After leaving the White Shark Research Institute, Michael came to an arrangement with the White

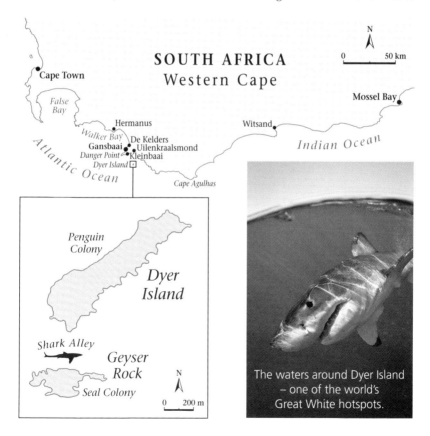

The waters around Dyer Island
– one of the world's
Great White hotspots.

Shark Diving Company in Gansbaai. He would be allowed to continue his photo ID work from their boat in return for working for them and helping with their cage-diving visitors.

Life on the cage-diving boats was different in Gansbaai in those days. There were far fewer cage-diving visitors, and most were shark enthusiasts rather than tourists. Instead of today's two or three trips per day, there was only one, often lasting all day. This meant there was plenty of time for Michael to do his ID work, and his database of photos grew rapidly.

Later, he expanded his research efforts by setting up his own NGO called The White Shark Trust, and during this period he operated his own dedicated research boat called *Lamnidae*.

To the southeast of Gansbaai there is a beautiful long, sandy beach that Michael calls Haaibaai. In 1998 the locals rarely used this beach for swimming, but to someone who grew up in landlocked Switzerland, the lure of the sea, the beach and the breakers was strong, and Michael often went there to swim and body surf.

On a day in early November 1998, high winds had caused the cancellation of cage-diving trips, but it was a glorious sunny day and so Michael headed for the beach.

That day there were no chum slicks to interest the Great White Shark and, while she would have taken a meal had one come along, she wasn't actively hunting. She swam through Shark Alley, between Dyer Island and Geyser Rock, and the seals watched her, preferring to keep eye contact rather than turn and swim away. The churning water at the east end of Shark Alley made the kelp dance crazily in the sunlight. She skirted the kelp, swimming above a sandy bottom, cruising slowly towards the faraway shore.

The beach slopes gently and Michael had waded over 100 metres out to get to the back of the surf, hoping to catch a ride. The surf was messy and not particularly suited to surfing, but every now and then a strong wave got hold of him and gave him a high-speed run for about

20 metres. He then battled his way back out and waited for the next one, standing in water up to his shoulders as he assessed the waves coming in and decided which one would give a good ride. The water wasn't warm but the exertion, the thrill of the strong waves, and the wonderful feeling of wild freedom made the temperature irrelevant. Suddenly, the blood froze in his veins: 10 metres away, a large shadow was approaching and swimming straight at him.

In summer, the beach area is favoured by sharks, but today the Great White had not encountered any other of her species, and hadn't seen any seals since she left the Dyer Island area. The only thing to interest her was her shadow on the sandy bottom as it accompanied her on her lazy cruise. Then her manner changed and she altered course. Her array of senses had picked up something interesting 200 metres away and she went to investigate. Great Whites are generally inquisitive animals, and this one was more inquisitive than most. She didn't hurry but she had to find out what was causing the disturbance in the water just outside where the surf started.

A large shadow
was approaching
and swimming
straight at him.

He was over 100 metres from shore and Michael knew he couldn't outswim the shark. His instinct said run, but experience and his knowledge of sharks told him not to panic. He called to mind the familiar theory: keep still and make yourself as small as possible. The Great White continued her approach. Michael wished he had tried to run: he was sure her mouth would open any second and he would be seized, turning the water red with his blood and becoming the latest shark-attack victim.

She came within touching distance and he could see her eye before she turned 90 degrees and swam calmly away. As the distance between them increased, Michael dared look round, needing to identify the source of a new booming noise; then he realised it was the blood pounding in his ears. He didn't hurry to shore – there was no need to, because he no longer felt under any threat. Back on the beach, the adrenaline was still pumping as he towelled himself dry. He felt exceptionally lucky and privileged: the shark had been only half a metre away, with Michael totally at her mercy. Yet alongside his fear had been a feeling of awe as he watched the most magnificent and magical creature he had ever seen. There was no-one else on the beach to hear him when he turned back towards the sea and said out loud, 'thank you'.

This encounter confirmed for Michael that sharks, and in this case Great Whites, are not mindless attack machines that inevitably maim or kill unprotected humans. Preaching this message was part and parcel of Michael's job, and was a mantra for all those working in shark eco-tourism. Now, to illustrate the point, and with the added benefit of personal experience, Michael would often tell the story of his close encounter with a shark – the very same Great White that would go on to become a celebrated icon in the struggle for the protection of its species.

As the summer of 1998/1999 gave way to winter, Michael continued taking photographs. The skipper of the boat on which he worked was Frank Rutzen, whose brother Mike would later become well known for free diving with Great Whites. Frank and Michael got on well and were a good team. Frank often stood in for Michael on cage dives so that Michael could pursue his photo ID work, which included taking notes about the sharks' sex, size and individual markings.

On a Sunday in mid-September, 1999, Michael was waiting for his regular lift to work. From his house at De Kelders, next to Gansbaai, he gazed out to sea, watching a Southern Right Whale as he sipped his coffee, and half listening for the engine noise that would signal Frank Rutzen's arrival.

Soon they were getting their boat ready in Kleinbaai, the little harbour on the other side of Gansbaai, before setting off to chum southeast of Dyer Island.

'I couldn't help thinking, if they had cameras they would have been photographing us!' (Michael Scholl)

Her dorsal fin immediately caught Michael's attention.

There were four cage divers on board that day: two Britons, an American and a Canadian. They had been chumming for less than an hour when the first shark arrived and, by 13h00 – three hours and four sharks later – the divers were 'sharked out'. They had had a wonderful experience and each of them had been in the cage several times. At first, excitement kept the cold at bay, but after so long, they were succumbing to the cold, and keeping warm now became an issue. Three of the four sharks had had their dorsal fins out of the water and Michael had taken good photographs of both sides of the fins.

Frank asked his clients if they had had enough, and the American answered 'More than enough man, that was great, the best ever'.

Like most Great Whites, she responded to the cage diver's chum slicks around Dyer Island; her sense of smell took over and, as if on autopilot, she swam up the slick to investigate. Sometimes, if she was quicker than the bait handler, she could grab a small meal – part or all of the tuna head. She would inspect the boat's hull and the human creatures in the cage, try and get the bait and then leave. The pattern today was familiar as she swam towards the boat, following the scent trail.

The divers were getting out of their wetsuits and Michael and Frank were starting to ready the boat for returning to harbour. Michael was about to get the chum in when he lifted his head and saw a shadow approaching from 40 metres astern. The shark swam upwards and the shadow became clearer; then a dorsal fin broke the surface. At just over 3 metres in length, the shark was unremarkable, but her dorsal fin immediately caught Michael's attention, and he went for his camera. The front edge curved backwards to a pointed apex; the back edge descended straight down and was marked by a series of distinctive serrations – a fin that would be easy to identify in future encounters. Michael's camera clicked as the shark made a couple of slow circuits around the boat, giving him shots from all angles. There was no bait line out so she had nothing to chase, and she left in a shallow dive. Michael wrote down '3 metres plus, female'. Neither he nor the Great White realised they had met before, or that today marked the beginning of a series of events that would lead them to make history together.

Michael, camera in hand, aboard his boat *Lamnidae*.

Today marked the
beginning of a series
of events that would
lead them to make
history together.

CHAPTER FIVE

New York

Before Ramon Bonfil joined WCS in New York in September 2001, he had been to the Indo-Pacific Fish Conference in Durban where he first met Michael Scholl. They met again at an International Fund for Animal Welfare (IFAW) meeting in Cape Town, and Michael invited some of those attending to come to Gansbaai so that he could take them to see Great White Sharks.

White Shark Trust

Invited by Michael Scholl (centre top) to Gansbaai to meet Great Whites are Peter Pueschel, Sarah Fowler, Ramon Bonfil, Lizzy Tyler and Rachel Cavanagh.

amon's first sight of a Great White was a defining moment. He was captivated by the animal's power, grace and beauty, and he left South Africa having made up his mind to find a way to get involved in researching them.

Two or three years earlier, marine wildlife researchers had started using pop-off archival transmitting (PAT) tags. These tags could be fitted to sea creatures, and were set to record depth, light and temperature information before detaching themselves, floating to the surface and transmitting data to orbiting satellites – their big advantage being that it was not necessary to retrieve tags in order to recover their data. Very little research had been done on the migratory patterns of Great Whites at that time, and Ramon felt that South Africa's sharks were an appropriate species for studying with the use of a tagging programme.

By 2000, the suspicion held by scientists and conservationists that sharks were being unsustainably overfished, and driven towards extinction, had become a widely recognised issue. Great Whites and other species that matured late and produced few young were of particular concern.

Soon after starting at WCS in 2001, Ramon heard that a wealthy young New York property millionaire, Greg Manocherian, was keen to fund research that would contribute to Great White Shark conservation. Ramon's fascination with Great Whites, the introduction of PAT tag data collection, and the possibility of funding all came together, and he set out to convince Greg that the best use of his funds would be to study the migration patterns of Great Whites.

The South African government had granted protection to Great Whites in 1991, and by 1999 these sharks were also protected throughout Australian waters. When Ramon first met Greg in March 2002, little was known about Great White migration. Obviously, if they were proven to be migratory and regularly travelled outside the waters of the countries protecting them, then their protection was seriously diminished.

Ramon's arguments were strong and Greg needed little convincing. If Great Whites were regularly migratory then Greg and Ramon needed

284   South African Journal of Science   Vol. 87   July 1991

Government protection for the great white shark (*Carcharodon carcharias*) in South Africa

L.J.V. Compagno

On April 11 this year the South African Minister of Environment Affairs, Mr Louis Pienaar, announced regulations for the protection of the great white shark *Carcharodon carcharias* (Linnaeus, 1758) in the exclusive economic zone of South Africa. The announcement was made at the South African Museum in Cape Town, with scientists and representatives from national and international news media in attendance. Apparently, South Africa is the first county in the world to pass protective legislation for the white shark. There is currently interest in similar legislation in Australia, and there is a motivation being prepared in the United Kingdom through the auspices of the Fauna and Flora Preservation Society to regulate the international trade in white shark jaws, teeth, and other parts under the Convention on International Trade in Endangered Species (CITES).[1]

The protective legislation makes it illegal to sell or offer for sale any white shark or part or product, and to catch or kill any white shark except on the author-

prepared a report summarizing the natural history and conservation status of the white shark locally and world-wide.[1] This was distributed to concerned parties while protective measures for the white shark were being considered.

The measures are seen by the ministry, and by researchers at the Sea Fisheries Research Institute and the Shark Research Centre that provided background data for the measures, as pre-emptive protection for a large, unabundant, poorly known apical superpredator[3] that has great notoriety, a high commercial value, and is the object of much negative human interest. The white shark is the largest species of the shark Family Lamnidae (Order Lamniformes), and the largest macropredatory shark. It is born at a length of approximately one metre and reaches lengths of at least 6–7 m and weights of over two tonnes. It feeds mostly on marine vertebrates, with other cartilaginous fishes, bony fishes, and marine mammals being its primary prey.[1] The reproductive potential of white

catches of commercial fishing gear in South Africa and elsewhere, but most white shark catches other than those from anti-shark nets are by sports anglers and commercial fishermen that target white sharks for jaws, teeth and fins. Such small fisheries are difficult to monitor because of their inconspicuousness, but can be very valuable. Prices up to R14 000 have been paid for jaws of very large adult white sharks in Australia. In South Africa, teeth and jaws of juvenile white sharks caught in the Natal shark nets have been sold locally and jaws of adult white sharks have been sold overseas.[1] While anti-shark nets in South Africa catch mostly juvenile white sharks, the more valuable adult sharks (3.8 m long and greater) are taken with heavy line gear.

Off southern Africa the long-term trends in white shark numbers are unknown and need to be elucidated. The only detailed and consistent statistics on white shark catches are from the anti-shark nets of the Natal Sharks Board, which yielded 22 to 61 sharks per year (mean 39.4) between 1974 and 1988, with a possible declining trend in catch per unit effort during this period.[11]

The objectives of the white shark research programme of the Shark

South Africa protected its Great White Sharks in 1991.

the evidence to present to the Convention on International Trade in Endangered Species (CITES) to gain an appropriate international protective listing for Great Whites.

Tagging sharks with PAT tags as a means of research was in its infancy, so Greg challenged Ramon to go to South Africa and prove that Great Whites could be tagged in this way, and information of value obtained. If Ramon succeeded in this pilot exercise, Greg would agree to fund a full research programme tagging South Africa's Great Whites. He allocated $50,000 to the pilot project – and Ramon's research dreams became a reality. He would need local partners in South Africa, so in early 2002 he contacted Michael Scholl and Ryan Johnson and proposed that they work together as a team deploying tags to research Great Whites.

Michael and Ryan advised Ramon that they would need both permission and help from the South African authorities, and referred him to Dr Herman Oosthuizen of the Marine and Coastal Management department (MCM).

The MCM marine research team working under the direction of Herman consisted of leader Mike Meyer, Stephan Swanson and Dean Kotze, with Ryan Johnson being involved specifically in shark projects. They were a close-knit team and were already involved in shark research deploying both acoustic and conventional identification tags.

MCM had the physical resources that Ramon needed: qualified personnel, ships, engineering resources, local marine knowledge, and some Great White Shark tagging experience. On the other hand, electronic tags – both PAT and SPOT (Smart Position or Temperature Transmitting) tags – are expensive, and MCM didn't have the money to buy the tags and further their research in this area; but Ramon had the necessary funding. He proposed the project to Herman Oosthuizen and Mike Meyer, and it was agreed they would work together, with Ramon as lead scientist, project leader and provider of funds, and MCM providing the permissions required for the research, and all the local resources that would be needed. A collaboration agreement was worked out and signed between MCM and WCS.

In mid-2002 Ramon left New York for Cape Town. He was now on trial; he had to prove conclusively to Greg Manocherian that PAT and SPOT tags could be deployed on Great White Sharks. The funding he so desperately needed to fulfil his research dreams was wholly dependent on a successful outcome of this first expedition.

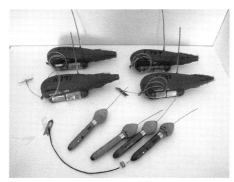

SPOT and PAT tags of the type
deployed by researchers

Ramon readies a tag
for deployment.

CHAPTER 6

Shark tagging on trial

*Ramon was now on trial; he had to prove
conclusively to Greg Manocherian that PAT and
SPOT tags could be deployed on Great White Sharks.
The funding he so desperately needed to fulfil his
research dreams was wholly dependent on a
successful outcome of this first expedition.*

Sardinops, the MCM research vessel

AT tags (see pages 57, 59) look a little like a singer's microphone and are about the same size. A short, flexible aerial is fitted to one end, and the fixing or anchor system is at the other.

On the pilot expedition, the objective was to deploy eight tags: four PAT and four SPOT tags. The PAT tags would be placed on the sharks while they were still in the water, using a spear type of device called a tagging pole. However, the SPOT tags (which, unlike earlier tags, regularly send recorded data to satellites) would ideally be fitted to the sharks permanently by drilling through their dorsal fin. This meant the sharks had to be captured and removed from the water, and it was over this that Ramon encountered his first problems.

He was working closely with Mike Meyer of MCM who insisted that sharks could not be taken out of the water. Great White Sharks had been protected in South Africa since 1991 and it was felt that removing them from the water would place both sharks and humans at risk. Michael Scholl felt similarly, believing it was unethical to take them out of the water. This meant that the SPOT tags would have to be towed alongside the shark once they had been positioned using a tagging pole, as with the PAT tags.

Ramon felt strongly that this method would not work but he had no option other than to try. Tagging was carried out in Gansbaai and Mossel Bay. As far as Ramon was aware, this would be the first time such tags were being deployed on Great White Sharks. Mike Meyer was a regular visitor to the tagging operations on Ramon's first trip, and he seconded Stephan Swanson to Ramon for the duration of the expedition. Two-metre tall Stephan soon proved himself invaluable; he had worked with MCM for many years and had built up considerable experience dealing with seals, dolphins, sharks and other sea creatures, large and small.

Between 10 and 28 August 2002, all eight tags were deployed. In Gansbaai, operating from Michael Scholl's boat, three PAT tags and one SPOT tag were attached; and in Mossel Bay, from an MCM vessel, one PAT tag and three SPOT tags.

Two of the PAT tags failed to report to the satellite at all, yielding no data; another lasted 11 days and the fourth stayed on the shark for 45 days. And, just as Ramon had feared, the SPOT tags stayed on for only a few days.

Ramon returned to New York at the end of August, feeling that the first expedition had, at the very least, been a valuable learning exercise. He had proved to Greg Manocherian that he could deploy the tags, and the fact that one of the PAT tags had stayed on for 45 days showed the application techniques could work, although they obviously needed improvement. He began experimenting on dead sharks with various types of anchors for the PAT tags, finally settling on one that he called an 'umbrella' anchor because, once applied, it opened and ensured a firm fixing.

In the first trial Ramon proved he could successfully deploy
the PAT tags; one stayed on for 45 days ...

Ramon was more convinced than ever that, given the limitations of PAT tags, real-time transmission data was vital for the success of the research programme. However, the failure of the torpedo-type SPOT tags suggested a change of tack was required: the tags would need to be fitted to the shark's dorsal fin, which would mean catching the sharks and taking them out of the water. The lessons learned on the first expedition were not lost on Mike Meyer, who agreed with Ramon that SPOT tags were essential. Discussions in MCM followed, and permission to lift sharks out of the water was granted.

According to Ramon, at this time only two researchers in Australia, John Stevens and Barry Bruce, had taken Great Whites out of the water.

... however, to attach the SPOT tags securely enough would require the sharks to be lifted out of the water.

They had caught a couple of small sharks, less than 2½ metres long, on hook and line and brought them into the boat prior to releasing them back into the sea. Ramon and the MCM team would be working with much larger sharks, and they started looking at safe ways not only of catching the sharks, but also of getting them out of the water so that the researchers could fit the SPOT tags and carry out other research tasks.

It was decided to catch the sharks with large baited hooks, making sure they got hooked only in the corner of the mouth which would ensure minimum damage and easy release. Once caught, the sharks would be guided into a cradle that would hold them while the researchers did their work.

Together with Mike Meyer and the MCM team, Ramon worked out designs for a cradle structure. The task of turning the cradle system ideas into a working mechanical reality fell to MCM's engineer, Michael

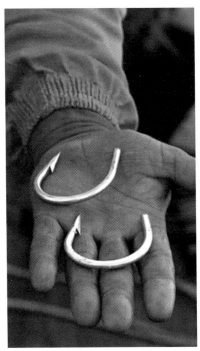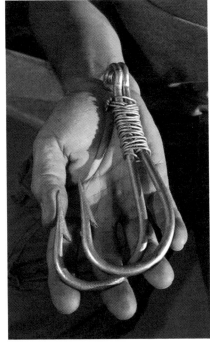

It was decided to catch the sharks using large baited hooks.

April 2003 marked the start of the full-scale tagging operation.

Patterson. During the southern summer of 2002, working in MCM's superbly equipped Cape Town workshops, Patterson experimented with designs, finally building a cradle structure he was confident would do the job. Over the years, Patterson's skill for invention gave rise to many original ideas to help the field crew carry out their research.

The structure he now built had a soft, flexible cradle for the shark to lie in so that its body would not be compressed. Once the shark had been guided into the cradle it was held safely and securely, and could be lifted out of the water and then lowered back again. Platforms alongside gave the researchers working access to the cradle.

Ramon spent the northern winter in New York and returned to South Africa in April 2003; this was the first of three trips that year and it marked the start of the full-scale research and tagging operation.

The catching gear
consisted of a baited
hook, a piece of chain,
and small and large floats.

By May, the cradle was in operation and so both PAT and SPOT tags could be deployed. MCM supplied their vessel *Sardinops* as the mother ship, and a smaller boat was also in attendance. Chumming was conducted from both the large and small vessels, but the general plan was that the sharks would be caught by Stephan and the catching team on the small boat, and then would be brought to *Sardinops* where Patterson had fitted the cradle.

The experienced team comprising Mike Meyer, Ryan Johnson, Stephan Swanson and Dean Kotze had worked together at the sharp end of marine fieldwork for years. Working at sea can often be dangerous, and even more so when handling big, strong marine animals. By now, all the MCM researchers knew each other's strengths, weaknesses and limitations, and knew they could rely on, and trust, each other completely.

Although Ramon was the lead scientist and, thanks to Manocherian/ WCS, the provider of the funds, he had to take his place in the team and earn their respect. Everyone was capable of swapping roles, but most of the time each man stuck to his own function, and they operated rather like a Formula 1 racing team at a pit stop.

Initially, Michael Scholl had been against the capture of Great White Sharks by hooking them and taking them out of the water. However, as the tagging proceeded and he saw the team in action, supported by veterinarians, he withdrew his opposition. There were two distinctly different operations, and they were never conducted on the same day: PAT tagging was conducted by the team working only from a small boat, but for SPOT tagging the sharks were captured from the small boat and then had to be guided through the water to *Sardinops* and into the cradle.

The team on the small boat usually consisted of Stephan Swanson, who worked the bait line and caught the sharks, or used the spear pole to deploy PAT tags; Dean Kotze, who was the chum master and also worked the bait line and took ID photos of each shark: and the skipper, who helped wherever he could. One notable skipper was Kevin Cox of the KwaZulu-Natal Sharks Board. Kevin was a great asset: he was very experienced around boats, was used to handling large sharks, and was more than capable of dealing with unforeseen eventualities.

For PAT tagging, the shark would follow the bait but not succeed in seizing it.

For both PAT and SPOT tagging, bait lines were used, often with a tuna head as the bait. For PAT tagging, the bait handler drew the bait through the water so that the shark followed it alongside the boat into a good position for the person with the pole to apply the tag. The idea was that the shark followed the bait but didn't actually get it.

For SPOT tagging, the shark was required to take the bait and get hooked. Once a suitable shark had been identified, Stephan would deploy his catching gear consisting of a bait line armed with bait, a hook, a small float and a chain on one end, and a large float on the other. Once a shark had been hooked, Stephan would let go and the shark would tire itself fighting the large float, exactly as had been depicted in the movie *Jaws*.

When anglers catch sharks and the shark swallows the bait before the angler strikes, the danger is that the shark gets gut- or deep-hooked. In this case, unless it inverts (coughs up) its stomach, it is unlikely that the angler will be able to remove the hook. If the shark is being released the angler has to cut the trace line, and the shark will be released with a badly ripped stomach, with a hook still in it; many of these sharks will not survive. The aim of catch-and-release anglers is to hook the shark so that the hook is accessible, and removal is therefore safe, quick and easy.

Sardinops was the mother ship and had smaller boats in attendance.

Stephan could make no mistakes and take no chances. He had to hook his sharks in the corner of the mouth, not only because good animal welfare practice demanded it, but also because a shark that didn't survive would be a waste of a $3,500 tag that would not yield any data. The aim of the catch team, the researchers, and the vets was to catch sharks while inflicting the minimum of stress, and release them as fast as possible with the tag fitted.

Initially, smaller sharks were caught so that the team could practise, equipment could be tried and tested, and methods perfected. Once a shark had been caught and brought to the main vessel, the scientists went into action.

Mike Patterson's cradle system in action

Ramon, Mike Meyer, Ryan Johnson and the vets all had their roles to play and were joined by those from the smaller boat. Ryan Johnson was often at the tail end of the animal, taking blood and DNA, and he soon discovered that the tail was just as dangerous as the mouth full of teeth at the other end. He was caught on several occasions by a powerful tail that catapulted him off the cradle platform.

The weeks went by and the deployment of PAT and SPOT tags continued in both Mossel Bay and Gansbaai. The weather on South Africa's 'Cape of Storms' seldom stays settled for very long, so work was often interrupted by enforced periods ashore, while the team watched impatiently from the shore.

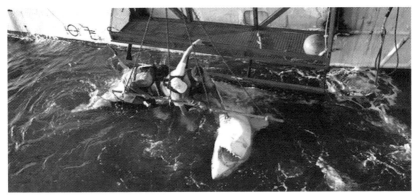

The aim was to catch sharks and release them as soon as possible, having inflicted minimum stress.

71

In 2003 the team
were pushing back
the boundaries of
shark research.

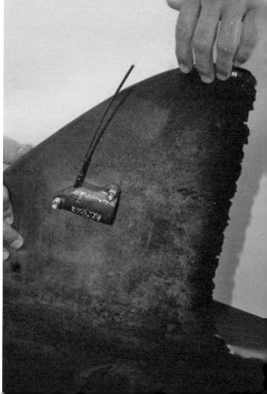

Friday, 7 November, 2003 is a date that, a few months later, would take its place in shark and conservation history. It had been over four years since Michael Scholl had taken his first photo of the dorsal fin of what he considered a special Great White. Over the intervening years he had seen her regularly and, perhaps irrationally, had come to think of her as a friend. He always recognised her; sightings usually started in early July, and would stop by the middle of November.

In the four years since Michael's initial sighting of her, she had grown over half a metre and was now an impressive animal. A creature of habit, she patrolled her home range of Walker Bay and the Dyer Island area for half the year, before she went on her travels for the other half.

Sharks are intelligent, display individual characteristics and have moods. On Friday, 7 November, the Great White was not in a good mood. Early in the day she had made a half-hearted attempt to catch a young Cape Fur Seal and it had got away easily. She then came across an injured penguin, which she caught and ate, but feathers, beak, bones and feet are not a satisfactory substitute for seal blubber, so she was still half-heartedly on the hunt as she headed towards the beach area from Dyer Island.

Due to her deeper draft, the *Sardinops* couldn't come close to shore, and was at anchor just over a mile offshore. Stephan, Deon and Kevin were aboard a small, blue-hulled, 18-foot boat with twin outboard engines, which had been hired locally in Gansbaai. Their chumming efforts had resulted in two sharks having been tagged earlier in the day. The first was at 08h46, just after they started chumming, and the second followed at 09h42.

Things had been quiet for several hours and Stephan's stomach told him that breakfast aboard the *Sardinops* had been many hours ago. He believes in Sod's Law, and decided that if he got his sandwiches and coffee out, then a shark would certainly turn up to spoil his snack. He was right. His coffee was balanced on a bench, and a sandwich halfway to his mouth when Deon said, 'Coming from behind, 30 metres'. The sandwich and coffee disappeared down Stephan's throat in record time and the team launched into their well-practised routine.

The shark swam up the chum slick and then veered off to her right to circle the boat on a tour of inspection. She swam at the surface for the whole circuit, and Deon got excellent photos of her dorsal fin from both sides.

She made a second half circuit, swimming about a metre below the surface, and then disappeared. Deon had swapped his camera for the bait line and stood at the ready, expecting her to come back up the trail and find the bait. Skipper Kevin also stood by to help in any way needed, and three pairs of eyes scanned the water. 'It's gone', said Stephan, seemingly stating the obvious, when Kevin said, 'No, look behind'. The shark had reappeared and was fast closing the gap between her and the bait that Deon had thrown into the slick astern of the boat. She was deceptively quick and Deon had to jerk the bait hurriedly up the side of the boat to stop her from grabbing it. The shark was moving too fast to change course and avoid colliding with the boat. She crashed into the steering gear between the engines, shook her head, and disappeared. 'Damn!' – Deon and Kevin spoke as one, and Stephan said, 'I don't think we will see that one again!'

The collision with the boat's steering gear hadn't improved the shark's mood but it had increased her wariness and her determination. She did three slow circuits checking the boat out from underneath. She could see the tuna head bobbing on the surface, and her sense of smell kept bringing her back into the area behind the boat where the chum slick was most concentrated. She had missed catching the young seal, had eaten only a small penguin and now the lure of the slick and the bait were irresistible. Speed had resulted in her collision with the boat's steering gear, so for her next approach she chose stealth.

'There it is!' Deon saw the shark first as she angled in towards the bait, gradually ascending in the water. There were two jobs to do: tag her, and get a DNA sample. Stephan was ready with his tagging pole, and Deon handed the bait line to Kevin, and picked up another pole he would use to get a small plug of tissue for DNA.

She appeared to be in no hurry, almost as if she thought that by going slowly she would be less visible. Kevin drew the tuna head carefully along the side of the boat and, now on the surface, the shark followed. She was in a good position and presented Stephan with a perfect target. His right arm rose and then fell as he drove home the spear that would implant the PAT tag. The impact was considerable but the Great White hardly felt it, so intent was she on the tuna head. Even though Stephan had used considerable force when placing the tag, there was no danger to the shark. The depth of penetration into her was limited by a hard, foam-rubber stopper. This ensured enough depth for the anchor to hold the tag on, but not enough for her body cavity to be pierced.

At this time, Dr Les Noble, a specialist in genetics from Aberdeen University, was visiting. He had a particular interest in the sharks' DNA samples, so that, although deploying tags was the prime aim, taking blood samples and collecting DNA, in addition to taking ID photos, were important secondary tasks. As soon as Stephan had placed his tag, Deon went into action. Using a pole, he stabbed the shark's departing back and collected a small plug of tissue.

The shark had failed to get the bait and she dived slowly away from the boat. She was unaware that she now carried a tracking device that would remain on her back, next to and just behind her dorsal fin, for the next 14 weeks until it detached itself. The device was a miniature computer that would record the depth and temperature of the water she moved through, together with the ambient light. With all this information, scientists would later calculate her direction of travel, the speeds at which she swam, and the distance covered.

And so it was that on the afternoon of 7 November, 2003, this particular Great White began her swim into history. She had not been named yet, but from now on was known to the scientists as 'Shark P12'. This reflected that she had been the twelfth shark to be fitted with a PAT tag during the programme. She would travel further and faster than anyone could possibly have imagined.

There would be more tagging the following year, in 2004, but the 2003 programme was now complete and Ramon prepared to return to New York. One evening before his departure, he and Michael were having a beer together at Michael's house in De Kelders while they discussed the achievements of the past few months. Michael was sitting at his computer, flicking through side-on dorsal fin photos taken of the sharks that had been tagged. He stopped and stared at a fin on his screen, a fin he was sure he recognised. 'I know this shark, I'm sure I know this shark!' Ramon got up and crossed the room to stand behind Michael and look at the screen. Michael's fingers whizzed over the keyboard as he searched for another image for comparison. 'There, that one,' he said, as he put the fins one on top of the other on the screen. They were a perfect match. 'I was right, I *did* know that shark!' The ID photo was dated 7 November, 2003, and Michael was right – it was his shark, now positively identified as Shark P12. He smiled and under his breath said, 'Now I may find out where you go every year when I don't see you'.

| September 1990 | November 2000 | August 2001 | August 2002 | November 2003 |

Michael was right: it was his shark, recently numbered 'Shark P12'.

CHAPTER 7

The long swim

*For the last five years, every November or December,
instinct had turned Shark P12 into a long-distance
traveller. And each year, the distances got longer.
She didn't know it, but she was following exactly
the same life pattern as her mother before her.*

ome years she went several hundred kilometres southeast into the Indian Ocean, and on others she cruised up the South African coast, passing KwaZulu-Natal's beaches en route to Mozambique, before returning to the Walker Bay area.

As with other migratory animals, she knew that at certain times of the year, instinct kicked in strongly and sent her on her journeys. She didn't go where she chose; she went where instinct and her array of sensory mechanisms guided her.

Her journey through life had started in the 1980s and, by the time she was tagged in November 2003, she had learned a lot about surviving in the oceans. One year she had been approaching shark-catching nets in KwaZulu-Natal and, just as she neared the net, attracted by fish that had already been caught, a boat appeared above her and she veered away. The men on the boat took fish, seabirds and a small turtle out of the net and discarded some of the dead unwanted creatures. She had eaten the discard before continuing northeast.

When she had encountered longline fishing vessels she was lucky that she had always encountered the boat first rather than the end of the line which often trailed several kilometres behind. The noise, the smells and the turbulence had always warned her off before she went for an easy meal already on a hook. She had once been caught in tidal beach nets, and fought her way free, before returning to deeper water, shaken but wiser and more cautious.

By the time she was tagged, her instinctive timer was starting to tell her to move. Instinct was also telling her to build up her energy reserves. The fates were on her side because, the day after being tagged, she caught, killed, and completely devoured a large but sub-adult fur seal.

She journeyed southwest, slowly veering away from the coast. Constantly guided by instinct, she knew with certainty in which direction to go. And as she swam, the device anchored in her back logged the details of her voyage; every 30 seconds the tag recorded light intensity, pressure and depth, and would later transmit the information to an orbiting satellite.

Every 33 seconds the tag recorded light intensity, pressure and depth.

On day nine, fate intervened and helped her again. She was swimming on the surface when her sense of smell told her of a meal in a westerly direction. She followed the trail and came across several dead but fresh fish floating on and near the surface. She wasted no time in filling her belly. She didn't know it but her opportune meal had been a tiny part of a trawler's catch, which had been lost over the side of the boat.

Shark P12 didn't know only where she was going; she also knew how she was going to get there. To the south of southern Africa, the Atlantic and Indian oceans meet, and where they meet a powerful east-moving ocean current system is created. The shark initially headed southwest from Gansbaai, and then turned more south than west. She held this course for her first 26 days, swimming on or near the surface, and then on day 26 she changed course and started heading southeast. She was hitching a ride on the east-flowing current system and, with minor diversions, her course would now be eastwards for the rest of her journey.

For centuries sailors have spoken of the Roaring Forties, some with dread, others with excitement, but all with respect. The Roaring Forties are between 40 and 50 degrees latitude south, and get their name from the incessant winds that blow across this part of the ocean. To the Great White it was just more sea and, although inhospitable, it was something she was well equipped to deal with.

Like Mako, Thresher and Porbeagle sharks, Great Whites are semi-warm-blooded. They have a countercurrent heat exchange system that is housed in a complex web of arteries and veins and is known as the *rete mirabile* or wonderful net. The system enables these sharks to maintain a constant temperature in parts of their bodies, regardless of the surrounding water temperature. This warm-blooded characteristic would now be one of the keys to the shark's survival.

For centuries, sailors have spoken of the Roaring Forties.

Peter Ryan

The Roaring Forties are colder than southern African waters and this temperature challenge increased when she started doing long, gliding dives to great depths. Her tag would later show that she reached depths of over 980 metres (over 3,000 feet) on her frequent dives. At these extreme depths the temperature dropped to 3.4°C, which meant that the shark had to return to the surface regularly to restore her body heat.

Relatively early in her journey, roughly 2,000 kilometres southeast of her home range, she passed Marion Island. The 19-kilometre-long island is the larger of two in the area, and is home to Fur and Elephant seals, King Penguins and others. Marion Island represented an important refuelling opportunity for the shark. Her meal of discarded fish had been a bonus which meant her reserves weren't as low as they might have been. Nevertheless, this was a feeding chance she couldn't afford to miss, as instinct told her that the next food source could be a long way off. Although not in a hurry, she knew she couldn't stay long. She ignored the King Penguins because she needed high-energy blubber to speed her on her way; this meant a young or sick seal. She set about hunting and on her third attempt successfully ambushed a Fur Seal from below.

The tag would later reveal that on her marathon journey, she spent 61 per cent of her time on, or just below the surface, and that she crossed the vastness of the Indian Ocean in almost a straight line, always heading east. To humans, the ocean often seems a wild, lonely, empty and dangerous place, but to the Great White, it was full of life. She encountered Humpback and Southern Right whales, and heard the faraway song of other whales. Albatrosses, with their more than three-and-a-half-metre wingspan, soared overhead, and sometimes when she was on the surface, they swooped down as if to greet a fellow ocean traveller. Fast-moving schools of tuna often crossed her path. She didn't chase them because she knew she had to guard her energy reserves, but she was always on the lookout for a meal.

Every dawn, the sun rose in front of her; during the day it passed overhead and then set behind her as she made her way eastwards. She may have used magnetic fields, stellar cues and other navigational aids, but providing the

Along the way, Nicole encountered – and feasted on – a dead Southern Right Whale, replenishing her energy reserves for the journey ahead.

sun came up in front of her each day she knew she was maintaining her eastward course. Ramon Bonfil later hypothesised that the shark's use of the sun as a cue may have been her main navigational aid.

She continued across the Indian Ocean, veering slightly north, and gradually the water temperatures increased. Unaware of national boundaries and protections, she didn't know that whereas in South African waters she was a protected species, in the open ocean she was vulnerable to the deadliest predator on the planet – humans. She was running a gauntlet with danger points all along the way. Longlines and fishing netters were frequent threats, and on one occasion she had a lucky escape when she bit the bottom two-thirds off a dead Blue Shark on a longline, and left with her meal, but without the hook. Three-quarters of the way along her route she encountered a dead Southern Right Whale, and gorged on it, fully replenishing her energy reserves.

Only a few hundred miles before reaching her destination, a fierce tropical storm caused her to dive to nearly 50 metres so that she could avoid the turbulence on the surface and continue her journey. As she neared the other side of the Indian Ocean, she had to pass through busy

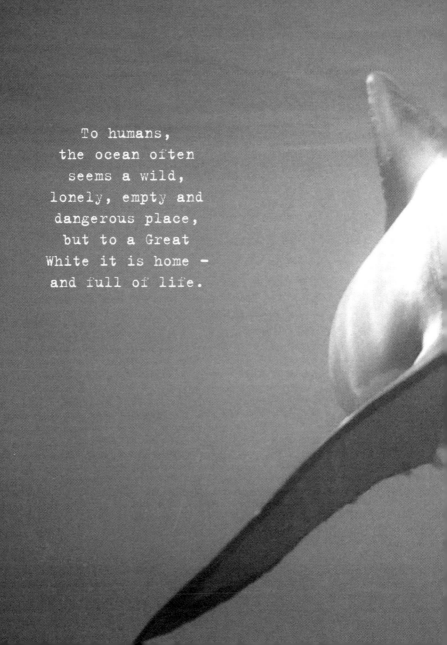

To humans,
the ocean often
seems a wild,
lonely, empty and
dangerous place,
but to a Great
White it is home –
and full of life.

shipping lanes, and avoid eating the discarded rubbish too often thrown from ships. Ninety-seven days after being tagged, she was entering a different world as she approached a famous coral reef.

When Saturday, 28 February, 2004 dawned, it was a typical grey New York winter's morning. Ramon was at home in his Manhattan East Village apartment. He made a cup of coffee and, taking care not to wake his partner Kerry, still asleep in bed, he took his coffee back to the bedroom and crossed to his desk by the window. A tag was due to pop off that day, so he checked on his computer to see if any results had yet been reported by Argos, the satellite company.

At the same time as Ramon was checking on his computer, Shark P12 was gliding slowly along a coral wall on a huge reef. In a few minutes, humans thousands of miles away would discover her journey's destination and she would be on her way to becoming a shark megastar.

On the Argos website Ramon went straight to the map that would show where the tags had popped off. Tag P12 had detached and was on the surface and transmitting. Ramon realised that he was looking at a map of Western Australia. Surprise, disbelief, doubt and elation were all emotions that swirled in his brain. Shark P12 was on the Ningaloo Reef off Western Australia; she had swum across the whole Indian Ocean! Ramon had harboured a sneaking suspicion that Great White Sharks might move between South Africa and Australia, and now his suspicion was confirmed.

Earlier intentions of leaving Kerry to sleep were forgotten as he leapt from his chair, gesticulating and shouting madly 'Kerry, wake up, wake up, you have to see this!' He hardly dared go back to the computer in case his eyes had deceived him, or there had been a mistake. There was no mistake.

New York time is six hours behind South Africa, so it was early afternoon when Michael Scholl got a call from Ramon. He was in the tower on his boat near Dyer Island, the wind was blowing, and he couldn't hear Ramon very clearly. Ramon explained that what he was about to tell Michael had to stay secret for the time being. Despite the poor line and the wind, Michael heard enough to make him want to shout and leap around. Instead, he bottled up his feelings and told Ramon he would call him later after he was back on shore.

Michael came down from the tower, put the phone down on the console in front of him in the wheelhouse, and told his volunteers that there wasn't much happening so they might as well weigh anchor and go home. Although Ramon had told Michael it was Shark P12, the interference on the line had been too bad for him to be sure, and he was eager to get to his computer and confirm the shark's identity. The volunteers were aware of some urgency as Michael sped to shore, then left, having forgotten even to wash the boat. On the short drive home Michael tried to keep his excitement in check but he had a peculiar nagging feeling that he couldn't quite understand; it was almost as if he knew which shark it was going to be.

Any doubt he might have had turned into joyous certainty when the computer confirmed it was Shark P12. This was his shark, the shark he had been photographing at the same time each year for the last five years. Michael called Ramon back, thanked him for the news and expressed the belief that the Great White would be back in South Africa and around Dyer Island by July or August. For five years he had seen her regularly between July and December before she disappeared again. Now he knew why she disappeared – she had been away on her regular travels, and he wondered whether this was her first visit to Australia. Michael's sighting records gave them both more than a little hope that they would see her again.

The two leading natural science journals in the world are *Science* and *Nature*, and Ramon knew that if Shark P12 returned, and he could prove it, he would be able to get the story published in one of the most prestigious journals in the world.

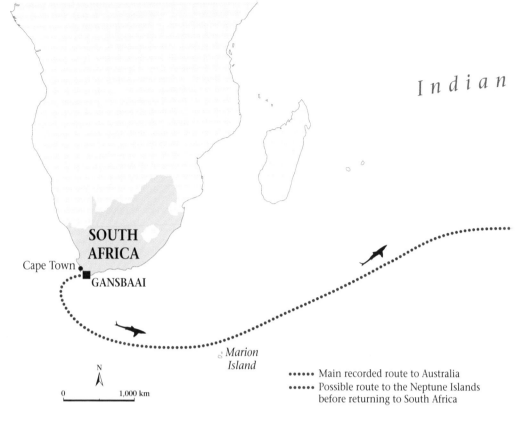

I n d i a n

SOUTH
AFRICA

Cape Town

GANSBAAI

*Marion
Island*

N

0   1,000 km

•••••• Main recorded route to Australia
•••••• Possible route to the Neptune Islands
before returning to South Africa

Hours later, Michael was still smiling as he lay in bed, waiting for sleep. He couldn't have been more proud of Shark P12 if she had been a child of his who had just won an Olympic Gold medal.

'His' shark, PAT-tagged on 7 November, 2003 off Gansbaai, South Africa, had swum 11,100 kilometres in 99 days to a point a few kilometres off the coast of Western Australia, south of Exmouth on the Ningaloo Reef.

She had travelled at a minimum speed of 4.7 kilometres per hour and at an average speed of 5.2 kilometres per hour. Hers was the fastest long-distance swim yet recorded by any shark of any species.

Ramon, Michael and the others were elated at her achievement. What no-one knew at the time was that she hadn't finished yet. By the time the story ended their shark would have further astonished the scientists, thrilled shark enthusiasts all over the world, and helped secure a safer future for all Great White Sharks.

Nicole's accurately recorded long swim would change
the course of history and help save Great White Sharks.

Hers was the fastest long-distance swim yet recorded by any shark of any species.

CHAPTER EIGHT

All the way to Australia

At the time when the tag popped off, neither Ramon
nor Michael realised what a stroke of luck had occurred.
The tag had detached at the pre-set time of 99 days.
Had the deployment period been set for 60, 70, 80 or
even 90 days, no one would ever have known for
certain that Shark P12 had reached Australia.

DIOMEDIA / Biosphoto / Gérard Soury

The sunny, shallow waters of the Ningaloo Reef were in stark
contrast to the conditions she had encountered for most of her swim.

blivious to her stardom and the luck that had helped create it, Shark P12 was enjoying herself. She had quickly replenished her energy levels on reaching the food-rich Ningaloo Reef. Whether the timing of her arrival was by design or accident, we will never know, but she had arrived on the reef at the start of an annual period of abundance and the emergence of new life.

The next full moon would trigger a mass coral spawning, which would see an extraordinary explosion of marine life and attract the world's largest fish, the Whale Shark. These giants can reputedly reach lengths of up to 15 metres, but pose no threat to other sharks as they are filter feeders (plankton eaters). They would have started arriving on the Ningaloo Reef only a few weeks after Shark P12.

The sunny, shallow, warm waters were in stark contrast to the conditions across most of her long swim. The seas she had reached were friendly in many ways, and key among these was that she was now safe again from man. The fishing dangers that had lain all along her migration path no longer existed here: years before, Australia had passed a law protecting Great Whites, so she could not legally be targeted in these waters. (A new culling policy introduced by the Western Australian government in 2014, however, posed a direct threat to Great White and other sharks.)

After a week on the Ningaloo Reef she started moving south, along the coast towards Perth. Most of the time, she was now swimming slightly more slowly than she had been on her ocean crossing. In shark terms, she was mooching along. Once past Perth, she turned east again and kept close to the shore, feeding as she went. Like the waters off southern Africa, Australian waters are home to a Great White Shark population, and along this coastline she came across other Great White Sharks. She welcomed the social interaction with members of her own species. By now she was nearly 4 metres long, and was larger than many of the Great Whites she met. Perhaps she was giving off pheromones, or perhaps there was something in her body language, but now male sharks seemed to show interest in her. She didn't fully reciprocate, but she often spent time in graceful swimming dances with male Great Whites.

Ruby-Gay Martin

In 2014 the Western Australian government introduced a policy of culling sharks to protect beaches. When the region's prime minister visited Cape Town in February 2014, protest marchers pointed out that Nicole had proven that South Africa's sharks were also Australia's sharks, so the Western Australian cull could be impacting on the South African population.

When visiting the Neptune Islands, Shark P12 found a cage-diving boat deploying a chum slick.

She reached the Neptune Islands, which reminded her of South Africa. The water temperature and marine topography were similar, Fur Seals were back on the menu, and her dalliances with male sharks continued. On one occasion she visited a boat deploying a chum slick, and found cage divers – and didn't disappoint them. In the clear waters she cruised around the cage for over half an hour, giving its human occupants the experience of their lives, and lots of wonderful photographs.

Not long after she arrived at the Neptune Islands (off the coast of Adelaide), Shark P12 started to feel restless. The same instinct that had sent her on her epic journey was now starting to tell her it was time to leave.

In contrast to what had happened in South Africa, the start of her return journey from Australia went unmarked by tags and the clicking of cameras.

On 25 April, 2004, she began retracing her steps, heading westwards across the Great Australian Bight. She passed Albany but didn't continue on up the coast past Perth and Exmouth. This time, there was no visit to Ningaloo Reef and she struck out in a west-northwesterly direction, heading back to the familiar coast of South Africa.

Not long after she arrived at the Neptune Islands (off the coast of Adelaide), Shark P12 started to feel restless.

CHAPTER NINE

Westwards again

Now the sun rose behind her as she headed westwards, and it set in front of her each night. She had left Australia's protected waters, and was heading for South Africa where she was also protected but, once again, in the middle lay thousands of kilometres of potential danger.

he reason Ramon Bonfil had requested Greg Manocherian to donate funds to the Wildlife Conservation Society (WCS) was to prove that Great Whites travelled outside the waters of the countries that listed them as protected species. Ramon's tagging programme had already shown Great Whites travelling to Mozambique, and out into the Atlantic beyond South African waters. The programme had achieved its aim of providing information that could be submitted to an international body such as the Convention for International Trade in Endangered Species (CITES) to get Great Whites protected throughout the oceans.

Shark P12's Indian Ocean crossing was an even more powerful piece of evidence that would be used to support this argument. If she managed to complete her return journey, she would further strengthen the argument. However, she no longer carried a tag that would prove what she had done, so if she did return to South Africa, which Michael's annual sightings indicated was a possibility, her achievement would go unrecorded – or would it?

Her return swim took a few days longer than the initial journey: she took a more northerly route in order to bypass the strongest of the currents that had helped on her outward trip. And, once again, she encountered natural dangers as well as those introduced by humans. She had developed a suspicion of large floating objects, an attitude that served her well. She knew now to be wary of any oil in the water, the throbbing of

Again, she encountered natural dangers as well as those introduced by humans.

95

Killer Whales (Orcas) have been recorded attacking and killing Great White Sharks.

an engine and all the other noise and pollution that humans cause, and to leave the area. Discarded rubbish from ships was a constant danger, and because sharks don't have hands or feet, which can be used to touch or feel objects to explore them, they use their mouths. Many times she had bitten into metal, wood, plastic, rubber and other substances to explore whether they were edible, and often now she didn't even bother with exploratory bites. If her eyes and other senses didn't indicate that something floating might be a meal, she mostly ignored it.

Halfway back she came across an American Navy aircraft carrier group doing exercises. The disturbance in the ocean was enormous; sonar, radar, engine noise, pollution and explosions had cleared the whole area of cetaceans (whales and dolphins), and Shark P12 followed suit, giving the ships a wide berth.

She cruised to the north of the fishing grounds she had come through on her outward journey, but other fishing grounds held the same hazards, and her experience and wariness helped her pass through safely.

Once, she was coming out of a long dive, returning to the warmer surface water to restore her body temperature, when she started picking up natural danger signals. The Killer Whale (Orca) is the only species in the ocean recorded attacking and killing Great White Sharks, and she now detected a large pod of Orcas between her and the surface. This danger had to be avoided, so she altered course and stayed deeper – and cooler – for longer.

She cruised to the north of the fishing grounds encountered on her outward journey.

As she headed west towards Walker Bay and Dyer Island, her mood would have been at the orange end of the scale.

She had built up her energy reserves before leaving Australia but hadn't been as lucky with food as she had on the first journey. She knew she had to sustain herself in order to make it home. Her luck was in when she caught an old Fur Seal. Whether the old seal was sick or whether she caught it off guard, she didn't know, but she came from underneath like an express train on full power and hit the hapless animal at 35 kilometres per hour. Having first disabled her prey, she circled, waiting for it to die before eating until she could eat no more.

We often attribute human emotions to animals: it seems an obvious way to understand their behaviour. As Shark P12 swam back into South African waters we would probably like to think she was happy because she had succeeded and got 'home'. Great Whites do exhibit individual behaviour and characteristics, and certainly have moods. Let's assume their moods can be measured from black to orange, with black meaning anger and annoyance, and orange meaning contentment. Then it might be that failing to make a kill and being hungry would be at the black end of the scale; fear of a pod of Orcas would be dark grey, and being in familiar waters with a full stomach would be orange. As Shark P12 swam along South Africa's familiar coast, heading southwest towards Walker Bay and Dyer Island, her mood would have been at the orange end of the scale.

Spyhopping is the action of poking the head out of the water to have a look around – behaviour that is commonly observed in whales and dolphins.

CHAPTER 10

World famous

On 20 August, 2004, Shark P12 swam along the familiar stretch from Dyer Island towards nearby Uilenkraalsmond beach and was unaware that she would soon be given a new name and would become the most famous shark in the world. And, more importantly, that she would become the talisman for a worldwide effort to secure shark protection – resulting in a CITES listing on Appendix II in 2004.

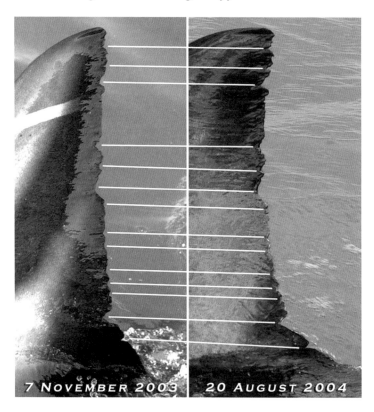

ompared to many other Great Whites around Dyer Island, she was now a large shark. On that morning, the Gansbaai cage-diving operators and Michael Scholl were all clustered around the Geldsteen end of Dyer Island. It was calm, with very little wind and, unusually for August, was quite foggy. No-one had seen any sharks; so, late in the morning, Michael decided to move and try his luck nearer the beach on the other side of Dyer Island. They moved towards the beach and, although no-one on board was aware of it, they passed right over Shark P12, who was 6 metres below them heading for the same area.

Michael cut the engine and anchored, while his volunteers went through the familiar routine of setting up a chum trail. A major part of shark research is waiting for the chum to do its work and attract sharks. It was an eerie, almost surreal day; the sun was trying to burn through the fog, but small foggy patches lingered still. As they waited for some action, Michael's volunteers chatted quietly among themselves.

Michael was in his favourite lookout position in *Lamnidae's* tower, holding his camera more in hope than in confident expectation. A patch of mist hung on stubbornly on their port side, resisting the efforts of the sun and light wind to disperse it. Something big, a long shadow, was moving along the edge of the mist patch and coming towards the

Michael was in his favourite lookout position.

101

boat. The shadow took on the clearly defined shape of a shark, a large one, then a fin broke the surface and the shark continued on its course. It was coming straight for them when, about 4 metres away, it turned towards the stern of the boat and presented Michael with a perfect side-on angle for photographs. His camera clicked rapidly on burst mode and he got several perfect shots of the shark's dorsal fin. He pressed the button to review the images and zoom in on them, and his hands trembled with excitement because somehow he already knew which shark it was. The zoomed-in images confirmed it: the trailing edge of the fin was unmistakable, meaning his favourite shark had not disappeared for good, but had simply been to Australia and was back again. And this time Michael wasn't restrained, letting out a yell of pure delight and excitement that might have been heard back in Australia. The volunteers thought he had gone mad. He couldn't say any more until he had spoken to Ramon Bonfil.

She stayed around the boat for two-and-a-half hours.

The real shark tale: Nicole makes record return trip from South Africa to Australia

By Steve Connor
Science Editor

A great white shark called Nicole has made a remarkable return trip from South Africa to Australia, setting a new record in transoceanic travel. Satellite tagging has revealed that the shark – named after the shark-loving actress Nicole Kidman – travelled 12,400 miles in fewer than nine months, and at one point dived to a record 3,215ft.

Scientists were amazed to discover female sharks made such long-distance journeys because until now females were thought to stay within the region of the ocean where they were born.

Ramon Bonfil, of the Wildlife Conservation Society in New York, said that for 61 per cent of the journey, the shark swam within 16ft of the surface, indicating that it may have used visual cues to navigate. "I'm very excited about the possibility that she was using celestial cues such as the sun or the moon," he said. "She travelled along a very straight track; she knew where she was going. It just blew my mind. Why else would a shark go to the surface in the middle of the ocean where there are no seals, penguins or other food? There is no reason unless she was trying to look at something."

Great whites may also be able to sense the direction of the earth's magnetic field, which they could be using as a compass for navigation, Dr Bonfil added.

The shark was tagged with a transmitter off South Africa in November 2003 and four months later, when the instrument was automatically released to float to the surface, Nicole was off the west coast of Australia. Data transmitted from the instrument to a satellite revealed her precise movements. The route is published in the journal *Science*. Five months later, on 20 August 2004, the scientists spotted Nicole back off the coast of South Africa, identified by the unique notches on her dorsal fin.

Dr Bonfil said the shark, who is sexually immature, may have been making a dummy run to find a mate in Australia where there is a large breeding population of great whites. "There is a possibility she does this regularly, maybe to find a suitable mate off Australia then return home to give birth in South Africa," he added.

The shark performed the fastest transoceanic return migration recorded by marine biologists, travelling for nine months at an average of three miles an hour, the fastest sus-

tained speed known among sharks, putting Nicole's trip on a par with fast-swimming tuna.

Sharks in general and great whites in particular are threatened by over-fishing and loss of habitats and the findings that they travel so widely suggest measures to protect them need to be global rather than local, Dr Bonfil said. "Our studies show the protection by a handful of countries – just five in total – is not enough if we want to protect this magnificent fish."

A second study in *Science*, by Barbara Block of the US National

Marine Fisheries Service, revealed that salmon sharks also migrating from Alaska to Hawaii. "Sharks are declining globally, yet the movements and habitats of most species are unknown," Dr Block said. Forty-eight salmon sharks were tracked from the sub-arctic with water temperatures of 2C to the tropics with temperatures of 24C. A specialised protein in their heart muscle allows them to live in very cold water which would interfere with the cardiac rhythm of other marine animals.

Nicole was tracked by her satellite tag as she swam the Indian Ocean twice, from South Africa to Australia and back, a total of 12,400 miles AP/M MEYER/SCIENCE

The voyage
The great white's 12,400-mile journey

7 Nov 2003:
Start of shark tracking

4 Mar 2004:
Tracking finishes

20 Aug 2004:
Shark is spotted

INDIAN OCEAN   Jakarta
AFRICA   UNKNOWN RETURN ROUTE   AUSTRALIA
Cape Town   TRACKED ROUTE   Perth
SOUTHERN OCEAN   1,000 miles

The Guardian | Friday October 7 2005   9

International

Bet on it **Sport**, page 32
How to beat the odds when
England take on Austria

»

Out of the blue Scientists track shark's 12,000-mile round-trip

Kate Ravilious

A great white shark nicknamed Nicole, right, logged more than 12,000 miles swimming from Africa to Australia and back in less than nine months. Researchers say it is the first time a shark has been known to cross an entire ocean.

A second report details the movement of dozens of salmon sharks from summer waters near Alaska to warmer winter quarters off Hawaii and Baja California. Both reports appear in today's issue of the journal Science.

In November 2003, Ramón Bonfil of the Wildlife Conservation Society in New York led a team that attached satellite tags to the fins of 32 sharks circling off the coast of South Africa. "It wasn't easy and there were some moments of drama," Mr Bonfil said.

Some tags contained radio transmitters that communicated with a satellite every time the shark surfaced. Others were pre-programmed to detach from the shark after a set period, float to the surface and send their data.

Most of the sharks swam up and down the South African coast, but Nicole – named after shark lover Nicole Kidman – headed for Australia, where her

Wanderlust

Route of the 12,000 mile round trip

South Africa   Australia

tag popped up to the surface. In August 2004, her distinctively notched dorsal fin was spotted in South African waters again. The results suggest that one in 32 sharks may have wanderlust.

Peter Klimley, a shark expert at the University of California, Davis, told the Associated Press there had been genetic indications that Australian and African shark groups might be connected, "but that's not the same as showing actual movement"

A group led by Barbara Block of Stanford University tagged 48 salmon sharks in Alaskan coastal waters and tracked them by satellite from 2002 to 2004. They found some sharks remained in the North Pacific all year, eating plankton in summer and herring in winter, while others swam south to Hawaii or Baja California in winter. As they swam south, they dove deeper into cooler waters, the researchers found.

"The shark heart slows down in the

cold, just as our own heart would," Professor Block said. "But ... where our heart would simply stop, the salmon shark's keeps on ticking."

The researchers found the hearts had high concentrations of proteins that control the uptake of calcium ions, which help maintain the heart's rhythmic contractions. It was the first time this has been seen in sharks, although Prof Block reported similar proteins in the hearts of giant bluefin tuna last year.

Michael's mega-decibel whoop of joy didn't disturb the shark. She stayed around the boat for two-and-a-half hours, almost as if she were saying hello, while showing off and providing photo opportunities. She had appeared dramatically out of the swirling mist and, as suddenly, she left. One moment she was there right beside the boat and then she had gone.

Michael saw his shark around Dyer Island another nine times and he noticed and photographed scarring near her gills, which he believes could have been caused during mating. The photographs proved that she had crossed the Indian Ocean not once, but twice. She was now the most famous shark in the world. Her journeys had given Ramon groundbreaking scientific data – all the material he needed to get her story published in *Science* or *Nature* as a scientific paper. Her story had appeared in newspapers and magazines worldwide, she was discussed in scientific circles and on TV chat shows around the globe, and was named after one of Hollywood's most beautiful movie stars: shark enthusiast Nicole Kidman.

During all the hype and excitement Michael carried on taking photos of Nicole, and was now talking to her and telling her how famous she was, and what she had achieved. He took his last photographs of her that October, by which time a conference in Bangkok had taken a decision that would greatly enhance the protection of Great White Sharks everywhere in the world.

The Convention for International Trade in Endangered Species (CITES) had been drafted in 1963 following a resolution adopted at a meeting of the International Union for the Conservation of Nature (IUCN). The text of the resolution was finally accepted in Washington in March 1973 by 80 countries, and on 1 July, 1975, the Convention came into force. CITES is an international agreement to which countries voluntarily subscribe, and its resolutions are legally binding on member states, which are known as Parties. CITES resolutions do not take the place of national laws, but each Party has to ensure that its domestic legislation reflects CITES resolutions and that they are implemented.

CITES is often wrongly thought of as a conservation organisation. This is not the case – rather, it is an organisation that governs trade in order to avoid extinctions and protect threatened and vulnerable flora and fauna.

CITES has its headquarters in Geneva, and in April 2016 there were 181 signatories (Parties) to the Convention. Every two to three years there is a Conference of the Parties (COP), and threatened flora and fauna species are proposed for listings to regulate or stop international trade in them. Levels of trade are regulated and defined by listing on one of three appendices: Appendix I, II or III. Appendix I is for the most endangered animals and plants, which are threatened with extinction; all international trade is prohibited, unless for scientific research or in special circumstances. Appendix II allows specific controlled international trade that is monitored by CITES to ensure the trade does not prove detrimental to the survival of the listed species in the wild. Appendix III is a list of species included at the request of a Party that already regulates trade in the species, but that needs the help and co-operation of other Parties to prevent unsustainable or illegal exploitation of the species.

Nicole's ocean crossings were events that would be included in the data submitted to the CITES Conference in Bangkok in October 2004. Proposals to list the Great White, Basking and Whale sharks had been presented to the Conference of the Parties (COP) in Kenya in 2000. For various reasons they failed, but Basking and Whale sharks were resubmitted to the next COP in Chile in 2002, and both species achieved Appendix II listings.

The proposal to list the Great White Shark in 2000 at the Kenya conference had been submitted by the Australian government. One of the reasons for the failure of the proposal was that it lacked sufficient scientific data. Greg Manocherian had financed Ramon Bonfil's research (under the auspices of the WCS) with one aim in mind – to get a CITES listing for the Great White Shark. In January 2004, in New York, Ramon convened a workshop meeting of many of the world's leading authorities on Great White Sharks, to pool all the latest information in support of the new proposal that would be submitted to the COP in Bangkok in October. The new information included results of the South African research that Greg Manocherian had financed. Ramon, Sarah Fowler, Michael Domeir, Michael Scholl, Ryan Johnson, Herman Oosthuizen, Andre Bustani, Alison Koch, John Stevens, Barry Bruce and others attended the three-day workshop. Out of the meeting came a report, which was submitted to the CITES Animals Committee in April 2004, together with a redrafted version of the earlier proposal from the Australian government.

In January 2004, in New York, Ramon convened a workshop meeting attended by many of the world's leading shark scientists.

Ramon was in a difficult position. Following the pop-off of Nicole's tag on 28 February in Australian waters, he knew he had made a big discovery. As an ambitious young scientist, he was keen to publish his findings as a paper in either of the world's two leading scientific journals – *Science* or *Nature*. He couldn't risk the fact of Nicole's swim becoming public knowledge or it would no longer be newsworthy, and his chances of getting a scientific paper accepted and published would be significantly reduced. He had to be very careful about sharing the news prior to submitting his paper.

Ramon's first submission was to *Nature* and he based it on the initial results of his South African research. It was rejected as being of insufficient importance and *Nature* suggested that Ramon try elsewhere.

He decided to resubmit his paper to *Science*, incorporating further data and the suggestions from *Nature*. His first submission to *Science* was also rejected. Then Michael Scholl confirmed in August that Nicole had returned to South Africa, and Ramon knew this information would greatly strengthen his chances of getting the paper published. He rewrote and resubmitted it, incorporating information about Nicole's return journey. He then had to wait patiently while his submission was assessed.

This was why, at the COP in Bangkok in October, Ramon was in a dilemma, because he knew that the full story of Nicole's migration would strengthen the case for a CITES listing, and would be a fitting tribute to Greg Manocherian for funding the research; but he also knew that if the story got out prematurely it could reduce his chance of getting published.

So he decided to compromise: he took his findings to the CITES Bangkok Conference, and called a closed-door meeting for delegates only, with no press or general public attending. He gave a presentation and told the story of Nicole's journeys, both outward and return.

The story was a powerful addition to the new proposal by Australia and the Philippines to get the Great White Shark listed in Appendix II, as was a socio-economic review by South Africa that probably helped sway other southern African countries. Nicole was something of a talisman for the co-ordinated group effort involving shark advocates from all over the world. This fell under the leadership of the Australian delegation, headed by Mrs Robyn Bromley who did a lot of the advocacy work.

CITES votes by secret ballot, and a two-thirds majority is required for success. Voting to protect the Great White Shark had failed last time; so this time, with new evidence, the stakes were higher, and the eyes of all those in the shark world were on Bangkok, awaiting the outcome. The votes were counted and the result was 87 in favour of listing the Great White on Appendix II, 34 against, and nine abstentions. Nicole and the rest of her species now lived in a safer world.

The CITES vote was 87 in favour, 34 against, with nine abstentions.

Nicole and the rest of her species now lived in a safer world.

CHAPTER 11

Why and how?

Nicole's transoceanic swim posed two different but related questions. Why did she undertake her epic journey? And how did she navigate so accurately? There are slight twists and differences in the opinions of the scientists interviewed in this regard, but in general terms there is agreement, and what follows is a consensus of their opinions.

The most likely reason for Nicole's journey relates to reproduction.

as her journey a one-off anomaly? This is highly unlikely, given the accuracy of her navigation, and previous scientific evidence showing very similar DNA found in some Australian male sharks to that found in South African animals, which indicates contact between Australian and South African populations. These two factors suggest that her journey was neither an accident nor a rare anomaly.

One reason for long-distance migrations in some species is to take advantage of a remote food source. While this is a possibility, it seems unlikely because South African waters are a rich source of prey for Great Whites. The Ningaloo Reef offers some different prey opportunities from reefs off South Africa's coasts, but south Australian food choices would have been very similar, and over 11,000 kilometres is a long way to swim for a slight change of menu!

The most likely reason for the journey is reproduction. In 2001 a DNA study carried out by scientists suggested that male Great Whites move between populations, and the best rationale was that this is to promote genetic diversity. The studies had established that South African, Australian and other Great White Sharks were distinctly different and separate populations, and research suggested that the females stayed within their home populations while some of the males did the travelling.

Nicole turned this theory on its head when she proved that females crossed oceans. Dr Les Noble, a leader in the study of shark genetics, hypothesises that she may have gone to Australia specifically to find a 'super male', a shark to which she was not even remotely related. This would contribute to genetic diversity and maximise the quality of her offspring. He comments further, as follows:

'My group has been using molecular genetic approaches to research the movement and breeding habits of Great White sharks for over 15 years. Our work suggested female white sharks mated with males from geographically distant populations, but gave birth where they themselves were born. However, we could not determine if males roamed and females were sedentary, or if females also roamed, but homed to their birthplace to give birth. Nicole confirmed that at least some, perhaps all, females

111

were as mobile as males but retained an intimate link with their nursery. This implied maximal outbreeding and remarkable ability to navigate to a safe nursery in which to birth the resulting young – in evolutionary terms this is a great strategy, provided the oceans change slowly. However, changes to en-route cues and local nursery conditions could have far-reaching consequences, so this behaviour could increase vulnerability in times of rapid change.

Given that we now know that females are as mobile as males, it follows that an errant female might establish a population in a new area. Genetic analyses suggest that Mediterranean Great White Sharks, which have low diversity and an Australian signature, may be recent (200,000 years or so) descendants of a very few antipodean females (perhaps even of a single female) navigationally bamboozled by anomalous ocean currents during a period of rapid climate change; eg an interglacial incident. The fidelity of first-generation Mediterranean Great White Sharks to their birthplace would shape the ecosystem within these new constraints. So, ironically, predisposition to long ocean swims and birthplace fidelity has in the Mediterranean provided perhaps the most endangered population of Great White Sharks in the world today, confined as they are to a polluted, crowded, highly exploited environment. Perhaps this will be an indication of the fate of other Great White shark populations?'

While reproduction appears to be the most likely reason for the journey, in some respects the scientific knowledge of the day seemed to contradict this theory because Nicole's age and size were thought to indicate that, at the time of her recorded journey, she was not yet sexually mature.

When Nicole was tagged in South Africa, an accurate measurement of her was taken, and she was recorded at 3.8 metres in length. At that time, it was thought that female Great Whites were not sexually mature until they were well over 4 metres. However, as Michael Scholl points out in a film about Nicole made by *National Geographic*, science does not know all the answers about Great White reproduction. Later studies by marine biologist Dr Greg Skomal indicated that these sharks mature sexually later than had previously been thought. Therefore, if reproduction was the reason for her journey, this would mean that at 3.8–4.0 metres in length, Nicole was probably over 20 years old, rather than in her mid-teens, i.e. she was some years older than had been assumed at the time of her tagging.

If pregnant females were moving across oceans from one protected area to another, it underlined the vulnerability of this species when, carrying their young, they ran the gauntlet across unprotected high seas. Nicole had made a major contribution to the CITES Appendix II listing of Great Whites and, in so doing, gave a valuable boost to the chances of others being able to replicate her journey successfully.

It is likely that in years to come, new scientific knowledge will conclusively answer why Nicole made her journey, but for now the most plausible theory is reproduction. One of the many things achieved by her migration was that she showed the need for further research. Starting in 2011 in South Africa, Ocearch (an organisation that generates critical scientific data related to tracking and biological studies of keystone marine species) carried out extensive tagging programmes, although none of the sharks tagged were recorded as having reached Australia. So far, Nicole remains the only certified trans-Indian Ocean Great White migrant, which may indicate that such journeys by this species are relatively rare occurrences.

How did Nicole navigate so accurately? Her journeys point to a sophisticated navigation capability. For humans to complete two ocean crossings involving over 22,000 kilometres of open sea, and be able to arrive at two precise destination points, we would require a whole array of complex electronic equipment. Nicole's equipment is all inbuilt; one day, shark researchers may understand exactly how she did it, but for now we can only theorise.

She spent 66 per cent of her journey swimming within 5 metres of the surface, most of the time only just below the surface, in the top half metre of water. This could indicate that she was using visual stimuli as navigation aids. On her outward journey, heading almost due east, the sun rose in front of her every day, crossed over the top of her, and set behind her. Just using the sun as a solar cue would have kept her heading east. On the return trip, when she was heading west, the reverse would have been the case.

Because she spent two-thirds of her time at or just under the surface, the use of the stars for celestial cues is another possibility. Research has shown that sharks use gradients in Earth's magnetic fields by which to navigate, and it has been suggested that this might be a reason for her long, deep dives.

It is perfectly possible, indeed some think probable, that Nicole was using all three cues – solar, celestial and magnetic – as navigation aids. It could be argued that there is nothing very precise about swimming due east and hitting Australia; after all, it is quite a large lump of land. However, Nicole's return journey indicates precision: she could have swum straight past South Africa and ended up on the other side of the Atlantic if she had been following only the sun. Instead, she ended up back in the exact same place where she had been tagged 9 months earlier.

While the navigation aspect of the journey was remarkable, so was the speed at which she travelled. Her minimum speed was 4.7 kilometres per hour, her average was 5.4 kilometres per hour, and her maximum speed was 5.7 kilometres per hour. This is the fastest sustained, long-distance speed recorded over such a distance for her species, and is comparable to that of fast-swimming species like tunas.

Nicole had blazed several trails: hers remains one of the longest recorded journeys of any Great White Shark; she showed that females undertake trans-Indian Ocean migrations; the speed of her journey is still the fastest recorded over such a distance for her species; her contribution to the CITES listing is a major factor in the protection of her species; she demonstrated precise navigational abilities; and she inspired further research.

Nicole's story challenges the notion of 'lifeless black eyes' referred to in the movie *Jaws*.

Nicole's story puts those 'lifeless eyes, black eyes, that don't seem to be living', referred to by Captain Quint in the movie *Jaws*, into a different perspective. Clearly, behind those 'lifeless black eyes' lies an intelligence that we are still striving to understand. Let us hope that Great White Sharks survive the current threats posed to them by us humans, that we stop demonising them and learn to share use of the sea, fully respecting them for the magnificent animals that they are.

Nicole knew nothing about the vote in Bangkok that further protected Great White Sharks, nor of the debate among scientists hypothesising how she had navigated. In early November, 2004, she left the Dyer Island area, heading east towards a battle that would test her courage, strength and endurance to new limits.

CHAPTER TWELVE

Shark-fin soup

*By the end of the mid-1980s, marine scientists and
conservationists had become aware of the threat to
shark populations. This threat was largely driven by an
extremely niche requirement – increasing demand for
shark fins in order to prepare soup for the burgeoning
middle classes in China and southeast Asia.*

he International Union for Conservation of Nature (IUCN) Shark Specialist Group was set up in 1991 and it has been monitoring and assessing shark populations and threats to sharks ever since. The demand for fins led to the advent of targeted shark fisheries in the early 1990s, and soon there was both anecdotal and scientific evidence in many areas of the serious depletion of shark populations.

Research dating from the year 2000, done by Dr Shelley Clarke, a fisheries scientist, was published in 2006. It is still often referred to when shark catch numbers are discussed. Her findings indicated an upper limit of 73 million sharks being caught annually for fins, and a lower limit of 26 million. Her 'best guess' figure was 38 million. Much higher figures are often used; up to 200 million is sometimes quoted. It is important to note that Dr Clarke's figures referred only to sharks caught for the fin trade, and didn't include sharks caught in other fisheries, or the large number of sharks caught but not recorded.

The transformation of the Chinese economy has led to an ever-expanding affluent middle class. This resulted in a huge increase in demand for luxury items that were not previously affordable, including shark fins. Shark-fin soup became a 'must have' status symbol on menus at events like weddings, other large family gatherings, and at state occasions.

Figures can be found to support most arguments, and so statistics must be treated with caution. However, most estimates agree that China consumes 90–95 per cent of the world's shark fins. Commentators also agree that the main reason for sharks becoming a targeted, rather than a by-catch species in recent years has been the rise in demand for fins for soup. Put these two facts together and it's clear that a major part of the answer to saving the world's shark populations lies in seriously reducing or eliminating Chinese demand for fins.

Recognising this, wildlife conservation campaigners from all over the world, led by WildAid, started focusing their efforts on China. WildAid began campaigning in China in 2000, and by 2011 had enlisted the help of Sir Richard Branson, Yao Min and other international figures, and was making measurable progress.

Low shark reproduction rates makes the impact of overfishing more critical.

Early in 2011, Chinese conservationist Jim Zhang joined with Ding Liguo of the National People's Congress (NPC) and Wan Jie of the Chinese People's Political Consultative Conference (CPPCC) and formulated a strategy: Liguo and Jie both proposed a shark-fin import ban to the NPC and the CPPCC. However, after the 2011 sessions of the NPC and the CPPCC, Zhang and his political colleagues realised there would be no quick route to a ban. Many sectors were involved, among them trade, customs, health, fisheries, agriculture and others, and Zhang realised the proposed legislation could, and probably would, get bogged down and take many years.

This realisation led them to readjust their positions and look for a faster way of limiting shark-fin consumption. According to the rules, if an NPC motion is supported by 30 congressional signatures, and a CPPCC motion by 50, they have to be fully considered and must be responded to. Both Lighuo and Jie secured the requisite signatures and made the same proposal to each legislative body, that 'Shark-fin consumption be banned from all government banquets and meals'.

This proposal was officially accepted and Zhang believes it will be remembered as a milestone in China's progress towards protecting sharks. The banquet ban was a long way short of their original target, but at least signified official government recognition of the issue. Since then, WildAid figures have shown a decline in Chinese shark-fin consumption. This can be attributed to a variety of factors including both WildAid's efforts and the banquet ban. As long as the downward consumption trend continues, this is a positive development for sharks.

Great White Sharks mature late and have relatively small litters of between two and 13 pups. This low reproduction strategy makes the species highly vulnerable to overfishing. The world has about 4,000 wild tigers and 25,000 wild African lions. Estimates for Great White Sharks vary enormously, with the highest being close to lion numbers, and the lowest being closer to, or even below that for tigers. The most frequently quoted guestimates are that the global Great White Shark population is between 3,000 and 7,000.

In 2011 a team in California estimated that there were just 219 individuals in California's most shark-populated region, although some disputed this figure, saying that it was too low; Dr Chris Lowe of California's Shark Lab believes the Californian population is, in fact, increasing and is a local conservation success.

Between 2007 and 2012, scientists working at South Africa's Dyer Island Conservation Trust (DICT) carried out a study involving Great White Shark dorsal-fin recognition. More than 20,000 side-on photos of fins were collected in the Dyer Island area. It took more than three years to complete the analysis, and 532 individuals were identified from the 20,000 photos. A computer program was then used to extrapolate the open population of Great Whites in the Gansbaai area, and the number arrived at was between 808 and 1,008. The previous estimate for sharks in that area was 2,000 so the DICT research halved the earlier number.

Australian research scientist Dr Aaron McNeil is optimistic: 'I haven't seen any evidence in the last decade that Great White Sharks are

Humans are not on the menu for Great Whites; attacks are tragic accidents.

declining. Yes, there is a historical depletion of Great White Sharks, but the story is not that they are going extinct. The story is that they are probably increasing very, very slowly.' (*National Geographic*, July 2016)

No-one knows for sure to what degree Great White Sharks are in danger, both because population estimates vary dramatically, and it is not known what size the global population was before depletion started. There is no doubt that in recent decades sharks, including Great Whites, have literally been in the soup! But Great Whites (partly thanks to Nicole) now have a degree of international protection as they are listed on Appendix II by CITES. Aaron McNeil and others believe there is cause for optimism, and many countries protect Great Whites from angling and commercial fishing. Nevertheless, the species is still listed as 'Vulnerable' by the IUCN on its Red List, and populations need protecting, as well as careful, continual monitoring.

Due to their iconic status, Great Whites have huge ecotourism value, and people travel from all over the world to the three Great White population hubs in Australia, South Africa and California to see them. In these places many livelihoods depend on ecotourism, and in the Gansbaai area of South Africa, in particular, Great Whites have transformed the local economy. It is not only the eight cage-diving operators who benefit; it is also local hotels, guesthouses, shops, taxis, restaurants and others.

Whether we have the right to exploit wild animals for human gain is a hotly debated issue. Nevertheless, in the case of Great Whites there is no doubt that their huge ecotourism pulling power provides a powerful protection incentive.

Scientific knowledge of these sharks is increasing all the time, and eventually we will know better how many there are in the world, and whether numbers are increasing or decreasing.

We all need healthy oceans for the general wellbeing of our planet. As top predators, both humans and Great Whites have ecologically important roles in keeping our seas healthy for the benefit of all.

CHAPTER THIRTEEN

After Nicole

*There is no doubt that the charting of Nicole's odyssey
not only informed scientists directly about many
previous shark unknowns, but it also inspired a wealth of
new research into shark biology and habits.*

Greg Skomal and
Lisa Natanson

n February 2015 a scientific paper coauthored by marine biologists Dr Lisa Natanson and Dr Greg Skomal indicated that Great White Sharks grow more slowly and mature later than had previously been thought. Their findings represented the first reliable growth curve for this species in the North Atlantic.

Natanson and Skomal believe that males mature at around 26 and females at 33 years of age. This means that if the scarring on Nicole that was observed by Michael Scholl related to mating, then she was older than was thought at the time. Slower growth rates and later maturity would indicate that population replacement rate estimates should be lower than those previously used. The new findings also meant reviewing estimates of the lifespan of Great White Sharks, as a lifespan of 70 years or more was now indicated.

Nicole's transoceanic journeys may have inspired some of the shark research programmes that followed. Information gathering and 'real-time' transmission tagging research was carried out in Australia, New Zealand and the northwest Atlantic, and an extensive programme was launched in 2012 by Ocearch in South African waters.

In March 2013 Ocearch tagged a female Great White Shark off Jacksonville in Florida. She became known as Lydia and, for a time, it looked as if Lydia might replicate the type of journey undertaken by Nicole and cross an ocean. She didn't make a complete west-to-east crossing of the north Atlantic, but her tag logged over 56,000 kilometres of travel, and showed her habitat to be the whole north Atlantic. Greg Skomal wonders whether the record of her movements might reveal nursery areas, and believes that the data gained from Lydia and others will help develop effective conservation plans for Great White Sharks in the north Atlantic. Like Nicole, Lydia dived very deep and her sensors recorded her at depths of over 1,000 metres. Perhaps Lydia and others tagged by Ocearch will contribute as much – or more – to science as Nicole; but Nicole will forever remain the first to prove that her species undertakes ocean basin migrations.

By the time the Ocearch programme began, information technology had moved on a long way from when Nicole was tagged in 2003. Now, not only scientists are able to follow the travels of Lydia and other Ocearch tagged sharks; shark enthusiasts anywhere in the world can log into Ocearch and follow the progress of these iconic apex predators.

Since 2003 there has been ongoing research on Great White population sizes. While estimates vary, it appears that their IUCN Red List inclusion as 'Vulnerable' is well justified, and this is underlined by the Natanson/ Skomal research on maturation and lifespan. The DICT population size research mentioned in the previous chapter indicated a local population of between 808 and 1,008 individuals regularly visiting the Gansbaai area.

Researcher Dr Sara Andreotti, quoted in *The Times* (London) on 13 August, 2016, estimated a lesser figure of between 350 and 520 Great

Whites remaining off South Africa's coast, with a breeding population of 333 individuals. 'This is extremely worrying because previous research on other species indicate that a minimum of 500 breeding individuals are required to prevent inbreeding', she said.

Andreotti worked closely with Great White free-diver and cage operator Mike Rutzen. They spent six years in the Dyer Island surrounds, collecting DNA samples and taking thousands of photographs of Great Whites. The DICT and Andreotti population estimates differ significantly, but even taking the higher figure (DICT: 1,008 individuals), the species appears to be under serious local threat. The Rutzen/Andreotti research on Great White Shark numbers using the Gansbaai area drew criticism from some in the scientific community. A collaborative response addressing these concerns was written and will be published in *Marine Ecology Progress Series*. Allison Koch is a coauthor of the response and she commented as follows:

A recent scientific study estimated that there were approximately 500 great white sharks left in South Africa. However, counting each shark is not possible and therefore scientists have to use indirect methods, often based on incomplete information, to estimate the population. In this case the scientists travelled to well-known sites in South Africa where great white sharks concentrate and photo-identified those attracted to their boat by their dorsal fins and collected a small tissue sample for genetic analysis. A complex statistical model was then applied to data from one of the sites (Gansbaai) to estimate the population of sharks using the number of identified sharks to those that were re-sighted. The problem with this approach is that the statistical model assumes that each shark has the same chance of being photo-identified. But, not all sharks present at a specific site are attracted to boats, and additionally, sharks at various stages of life use sites differently e.g. juvenile great whites are more common along the east coast, while sub-adults are more common further south, and male and female sharks segregate for some of the time. Therefore, collecting information at one site alone likely does not represent the whole population. However, the scientists tried to validate these findings by using genetic analysis to estimate the number of breeding white sharks. While these samples came from five different sites along the South African coastline over a four year period, it still excluded large sections of the South African coast where great whites are known to occur and they ran into the same problem as above regarding not being able to collect samples from all life-history stages. Therefore it is likely that their results are not representative of the whole South African population, but likely represent a proportion of the population instead.

In the 30 years between 1978 and 2008, it is believed that shark protection measures such as nets and baited hooks protecting beaches have killed at least 1,000 Great White Sharks.

Since Nicole's epic journey, science has answered many questions about Great White Sharks, but there are still enormous gaps in our knowledge. When Ramon Bonfil and his colleagues were conducting research in 2003, there was little co-operation or collaboration between South African researchers. By 2016 collaborative research had become the established norm in South Africa and, as a result, our understanding of Great White Sharks is increasing and the holes in our knowledge are being filled in.

Since *Science* published Bonfil's paper on Nicole in 2003, researchers around the world have published a considerable body of work. In 2010, the International White Shark Symposium met in Hawaii, and a full list of the scientists who attended encompasses most of the leading researchers in the world. Readers who are keen to know the detail of 'post-Nicole' Great White Shark research can obtain the list of attendees, and gain access to their research via the internet.

In view of the proliferation of knowledge and information now available about Great White Sharks and other marine life, it is worth noting that, without robust conservation measures being rigorously enforced, research can potentially be a double-edged sword. On the one hand, knowledge is required to effectively protect species; but on the other hand, once there are no secrets left, the work of poachers and other illegal catchers becomes easier. Only sustained and conscientious vigilance can safeguard species as precariously positioned as the Great White Shark.

CHAPTER FOURTEEN

The future of sharks

Oceans without sharks, without Great White Sharks, wouldn't be as healthy. If the 'new kids on the block' cause this to happen, it is unlikely the planet will forgive us.

uoted in an article in the *London Times* on 13 August, 2016, Mike Rutzen and Sara Andreotti (see chapter 13) do not present an optimistic view for the future of Great White Sharks in South African waters. Rutzen says, 'You used to go out on a cage-diving trip and it was normal to see 20 Great Whites. Today you are lucky if you see two or three. The number of sharks is dropping and I think in the years ahead there is a good chance they will be extinct. For years they've been wiped out by shark nets, baited hooks, poachers looking for jaws as trophies, and fins that are sent to the eastern countries as a delicacy. They have also been hit by a fall in their food supply. Now they are on the verge of extinction. In three years from now, I doubt there will be many Great Whites left along the South African coastline.' Andreotti says, 'Our hope is that from now on Great White Sharks will be monitored more closely and that better protection measures will be put in place.' Rutzen adds, 'There are a number of things we can do immediately to help the sharks. The authorities can ban nets and baited hooks, and CITES (Convention on International Trade in Endangered Species) can raise Great Whites from an Appendix II animal to an Appendix I to give it more protection. We need to involve everyone in studying and helping Great Whites. While everyone is working on their own, our king of the oceans could be on the brink of extinction.' In fact, there is now considerable collaboration among South African Great White researchers.

Population estimates may vary, and Chris Lowe (California) and Aaron MacNeil (Australia) are more optimistic than others. But what no-one doubts is that there is cause for concern. The species is threatened, and careful management and effective conservation measures are needed to ensure the survival of the Great White Shark.

In one form or another, sharks have been on planet Earth for 400–450 million years. Humans, in our modern form, have been on the planet for only 200,000 years. Compared to sharks, we have been here five minutes, and there is an unjust irony that the 'new kids on the block' are forcing many of Earth's much older inhabitants towards extinction. Natural cycles and events have always caused extinctions, and sometimes mass extinctions. However, it is only relatively recently that man-made extinctions started to be recorded.

Sharks of the World, published by Wild Nature Press in 2013, listed over 500 different species. Previously, in 2005, the HarperCollins *Field Guide to the Sharks of the World* had listed over 450 species. Ninety species are listed in the 2013 book that didn't appear in the 2005 guide. New species are being discovered all the time, and it is almost certain that some species will go extinct before being recorded by science.

Human-wildlife conflict (HWC) is usually associated with land species such as elephants competing with humans for space, and with land-based apex predators like lions, tigers and crocodiles, which kill humans. However, a continually increasing human population, combined with inventions such as the wet suit, mean more people each year are using the sea for recreation. This has increased HWC between sharks and humans, and will continue to do so.

If a human visits an African game park, ignores the advice to stay in the car, and as a result gets killed by a lion, the human is labelled as having been stupid, and the lion is only rarely blamed for having behaved like a lion – such incidents appear to be more readily excused and understood by people

Bathers frequenting beaches known to be patrolled by dangerous sharks have invaded the sharks' territory, and may well attract their attention. In the event of an attack by a shark, the animal is blamed, demonised and perhaps even hunted down by enraged and frightened humans.

If we are to share the seas with sharks and coexist without conflict, we must learn to respect the ocean's apex predators, and acknowledge that, when using the sea to play in, we have entered their domain; we have 'got out of our cars'.

Clearly, using strong-arm measures to protect beaches is one of the factors threatening sharks' survival; it is also arrogant and unfair. Shark spotters, non-fatal barrier nets and common sense are measures that can go a long way towards keeping water users safe in areas where dangerous sharks are present. In order to coexist successfully with sharks, we have to acknowledge that we are the interlopers, and understand that the price we have to pay for invading their space will occasionally be tragic accidents.

Ideally, humankind needs a 'road to Damascus' awakening, where we acknowledge that we are not the only animals that have a right to live on this planet. We don't have God-given dominion to destroy all other species, and we must let wildlife continue to be wild, and give wild creatures, both on land and in the sea, space in which to live their wild lives.

For a healthy planet we need healthy oceans. Healthy oceans need properly functioning ecosystems, and ecosystems only function properly and successfully when apex predators are present. Sharks are a vital component of ocean ecosystems, and self-interest alone should make us want to conserve viable shark populations.

By 2020 we will have lost 67% of the wildlife that existed on earth in 1975.
WWF/ZSL

Epilogue

Nicole was two miles south of Cape Agulhas, swimming slowly eastwards. She was close to the route she had followed years before, when she journeyed up South Africa's coast heading in the direction of Mozambique. Satellite and identification tagging had later established this as a well-used route for Great White Sharks.

lthough Great Whites are protected in South African waters, there are still unscrupulous skippers who are prepared to break the law and take thrill-seeking anglers out to catch these apex predators. If you know where to look or to whom to talk, it isn't difficult for 'sportsmen' to buy the chance to go and catch one of the ocean's supreme prizes. That Great White Sharks are an endangered species, and being hunted and caught would inflict considerable stress and a high chance of internal damage and cruelty, doesn't concern the trophy seekers.

There was a slight chill in the early-morning air in the little harbour at Struisbaai, just after 06h00, as the skipper, his helper and their two clients went aboard the angling vessel and made ready to depart. The anglers had travelled all the way from Europe with the aim of catching a Great White Shark. If they were asked to justify their actions, the skipper and his crewman would have said they were catching sharks for 'research', and the anglers would have described themselves as 'sportsmen'.

The 10-metre boat was rigged for sports fishing and was equipped with holders for rods, and a 'fighting chair' bolted into the clear deck space at the stern. Out at sea it was still only 07h00, but the chill of an hour ago had gone and soon the sun would push the temperature to over 30ºC. They were sipping coffee as they headed southeast to a mark where they would shut down the engines, put out their chum lines and start drifting.

Nicole's path would intersect with that of the angling vessel. History was repeating itself in the cruellest of ironies as she headed for the same battle that her mother had fought and lost many years ago.

It could have been a scene from the movie *Jaws*. One of the clients was half asleep in the fighting chair, his friend was reading an angling magazine, and the skipper and his mate were talking quietly in the wheelhouse. The boat was drifting on an almost flat sea and when there was any wind it was a welcome and cooling relief from the heat.

She flew through the air then
crashed back into the water with
a huge splash and was gone.

Unlike in *Jaws*, however, the 130-lb (60-kg) line didn't make a couple of faint clicks on the reel; instead, it suddenly pulled tight in an initial run, before screaming out, pulled by Nicole as she fled, seeking freedom. The skipper had used a small live shark as bait, and the angler had learned to ignore the little movements on the line as the shark bait swam in small circles.

Nicole had swum up many chum lines in her life and chased many baits near boats. Today was no different – or was it? She had responded to the scent trail and found a live shark on a hook. Something made her wary and she circled the bait twice before going in to attack it. The initial run of line off the reel had not been Nicole; it had happened when the small shark saw her and stopped swimming in its slow circle, panicked and tried to swim away. This excited Nicole who went straight after it in attack mode, then hit and swallowed it before realising something was wrong and taking off. She felt the pressure of the steel trace as she swam off, eating the shark as she went. The pressure in her mouth was then joined by a sharp stab in her gut as the hook caught in her flesh.

The skipper leapt into action, quickly crossed to his client, strapped him into the fighting harness and positioned the rod. The angler had come out of his half-sleep as if struck by lightning, and was now following the skipper's instructions while shaking with excitement and anticipation.

'Is it a Great White?'

'Ja, I think so; let it run for a count of five, and then as soon as you are ready, strike the fish and set the hook nice and deep.'

The client stopped the reel running and pulled back, which was when Nicole felt the stab in her stomach.

For over an hour man fought shark, and twice the angler managed to reel Nicole back in and close enough to the boat to be seen by all those aboard. On one occasion her distinctive fin broke the surface, before she was off again as the angler cursed and swore. One of his hands bled and his arms ached, and he wondered who would win. The line was slack but this didn't concern him, it had gone slack before and had been a prelude to Nicole making another mighty run in her bid to escape.

Truly wild creatures probably don't feel fear in the same way that humans and tame, habituated animals do. For wild creatures there is life, struggle for survival and death. Nicole did not know what had happened and was not afraid; she was solely occupied with getting away and surviving. Several times she allowed herself, unresisting, to be dragged through the water towards the boat as the angler reeled her in. She saved her strength until she was near to the boat and then sped off again, racing for freedom. With each run both she and her captor got a little more tired, and for both of them the pain increased.

This was a battle of wills rather than a test of strength and it was a battle Nicole had to win. She was now being dragged through the water again and the pain in her gut was intense. She was tiring but instinct ensured she kept fighting. Very slowly, she dived deeper and slightly towards the boat and as she did so, the line slackened.

The angler was puzzled. The shark had previously run and he had reeled in, and then it had run again, and he had reeled in; this had happened repeatedly. Somehow, this felt different and his brow furrowed in a worried frown: 'I think she is tired now; I will have her this time'.

The line seemed slacker and he reeled in a little to make sure she was still there. Nicole felt the line and something happened, it was like a switch being flipped in her brain – she charged fast, straight at the boat.

The line was now really slack as Nicole swam at the boat and the angler reeled in as fast as he could. He couldn't keep up with the shark and the line was still slack as she dived under the boat. As she passed under the hull, the line caught on the propeller and then tightened when she took up the slack. The heavy-duty line parted like spaghetti and immediately the stabbing pain in Nicole's gut lessened in intensity.

The angler sat, stunned, while the skipper swore.

A minute or so later the four men were discussing what had happened, and were all looking in the same direction when Nicole burst from the water 150 metres off their port side. She flew through the air then crashed back into the water with a huge splash and was gone.

As soon as the line was cut, the pressure in Nicole's mouth disappeared and the sharp pain in her gut was replaced by a dull ache. As she sped away from the boat and from the source of her suffering, the steel trace and the monofilament line trailed from her mouth. She dived and then raced to the surface where she leapt out of the water in a full clear breach before splashing back onto her stomach, trying to rid herself of the ache in her gut.

Still trailing the evidence of her capture she dived, heading for the comfort and safety of the deep.

Acronyms

CITES – Convention on International Trade in Endangered Species of Wild Fauna & Flora

COP – Conference of the Parties (CITES)

CPPCC – Chinese People's Political Consultative Conference

DICT – Dyer Island Conservation Trust

HWC – Human-wildlife conflict

ICCAT – International Commission for the Conservation of Atlantic Tunas

ICES – International Council for the Exploration of the Seas

IFAW – International Fund for Animal Welfare

IWSS – International White Shark Symposium

IUNC – International Union for the Conservation of Nature

MCM – Marine and Coastal Management

NPC – National People's Congress

PAT – Pop-off archival tag

SOSF – Save Our Seas Foundation

WCS – World Conservation Society

Useful websites

American Elasmobranch Society – www.elasmo.org
Dyer Island Conservation Trust (DICT) – www.dict.org.za
Elasmo.com – www.elasmo.com
Fishbase – www.fishbase.org
KwaZulu-Natal Sharks Board – www.shark.co.za
International Shark Attack File – www.flmnh.ufl.edu/fish/isaf/home
Project AWARE – www.projectaware.org
Reef Quest Centre for Shark Research – www.elasmo-research.org
Richard Peirce – www.peirceshark.com
Save Our Seas Foundation – www.saveourseas.com
Sea Shepherd – www.seashepherd.org
Shark Angels – www.sharkangels.org
Shark Conservation Society – www.sharkconservationsociety.com
Shark Research Institute – www.sharks.org
Sharksavers – www.sharksavers.org
Shark Spotters – www.sharkspotters.org
Shark Trust – www.sharktrust.org
Sharkwatch – www.shark-watch.com
WildAid – www.wildaid.org
WWF – www.worldwildlife.org

NOTE: The following link gives access to the scientific paper that was published in *Science* and described Nicole's 'Long Swim':
http://science.sciencemag.org/content/310/5745/100